TOWN AND COUNTRY

I0091195

THE UNIVERSITY OF NORTH CAROLINA
SOCIAL STUDY SERIES

———◆◄●►◆———

The University of North Carolina Press
Chapel Hill, N. C.

The Baker and Taylor Co.
New York

Oxford University Press
London

Maruzen-Kabushiki-Kaisha
Tokyo

TOWN
AND
COUNTRY

By ELVA E. MILLER

LATE EDITOR OF THE *SOUTHERN AGRICULTURIST*

CHAPEL HILL

THE UNIVERSITY OF NORTH CAROLINA PRESS

1928

COPYRIGHT, 1928, BY
THE UNIVERSITY OF NORTH CAROLINA PRESS

PRINTED IN THE UNITED STATES OF AMERICA BY
THE SEEMAN PRESS, DURHAM, NORTH CAROLINA

THIS BOOK WAS DIGITALLY PRINTED.

FOREWORD

Written as it was, after the relentless malady which finally claimed his life had begun to take toll of his strength and make his every effort a source of pain, this book is the capsheaf of the rich store of writing in the interest of a better, broader country life in America which constitutes the published work of the author. That the end came before he could see this final, studious, affectionate expression on a subject so close to his heart take book form is one of those tragedies to which men are too often forced to submit, whose lives are dedicated to the welfare of the many rather than the enrichment of the few.

Elva E. Miller was country born and, although he had worked in cities and enjoyed travel in his own and foreign lands, he remained a country-minded man. By which nothing suggesting provincialism or narrowness is meant. Although his work as chief editor of the Southern Agriculturist for many years made his devotion to his native Tennessee and her sister states of the South a growing passion in him, there was in his writings no hint of a selfish sectionalism. Every tiller of the soil was his brother and the small town dweller his next-of-kin.

To a reader of this book in manuscript, who had never seen the author, it seemed "he was very clear sighted, very kindly, and that the welfare of country and town in association with each other must have been a peculiarly dear subject." It was. The pages that follow are but a crystallization of thoughts expressed in articles, pamphlets, and letters through many years of devotion to this and kindred subjects.

Country-minded he was, but in a national sense. Early in life he realized that the farm was as much affected by taxation, foreign policies, the tariff, development of national resources, transportation, flood control, and all the problems of national government as were factories, stores, and city property. Education to him meant not merely colleges and central high schools, but more poignantly, the placing of at least eight months of improved teaching within reach of every rural child.

To the study of these and other great subjects he brought a mind of rare native clarity reinforced by continuous study of the kind which springs from deep interest and not from prodding. Clear thinking, indeed, was his supreme possession and with it went that rare added sense, prophetic vision, of which the reader will find many evidences in this present volume.

B. KIRK RANKIN.

NASHVILLE, TENNESSEE,
December, 1927.

PREFACE

The problems of the farmer and the farming districts have been engaging the attention of many thoughtful people these latter years. Both countrymen and townsmen have been asking themselves— or have been trying to tell others—what the country districts must do, or have done for them, if they are to be saved from poverty and stagnation. Similarly, the problems of the city and of city life are being wrestled with by many who have become concerned about the city's future. The particular problems of the small town, even, have come in for their share of consideration. Yet, in all these studies small consideration, apparently, has been given to the distinctively country town and to its relationship with the country about it.

This little book is primarily a study of the town in the country; secondarily, a study of the country about the town. The writer believes that the country town can be truly seen only against its unescapable background of fields and farmhouses and farming folk. He believes, too, that much discussion of agriculture and agricultural problems has been inadequate because it has stopped with the end of the farming lands and at the boundaries of the town. The country has been thought of, and treated, as one entity, the town as another, when, as a matter of fact, they are joined together as inseparable parts of one economic unit. They can not be put apart either in activities or in interests. The concerns of one are inevitably the concerns of the other. Opposing ideas and interests they may have; but always more of mutuality than of opposition.

Written frankly from a countryman's point of view, the book is addressed primarily to the townsman. The author hopes, of course, that it will not be without interest to the farmer and the agricultural leader; but his chief desire has been to tell progressive and forward-looking townsmen some of the things a countryman sees and thinks when he looks toward town and considers the meaning of the town to him and his fellows.

In a word, it is a plea for a better understanding between town and country and an attempt to promote that understanding—a little message and a call of greeting from the fields to the many thousands of thoughtful persons who are these days looking out from the marts and the streets toward the open spaces that surround both street and mart.

E. E. MILLER.

CONTENTS

TOWN AND COUNTRY

Chapter I

THE TOWN IN THE COUNTRY

WHAT IS A COUNTRY TOWN?

A country town, as it will be understood in these pages, is any town situated in an agricultural region and drawing its sustenance from—which means doing its business with—the country. The definition is elastic; it is also indefinite. But rigid definition would of necessity be inaccurate, and any attempt to say just what size or type of town should be regarded as something else, would be futile. Some little hamlets are not country towns; their interests and connections are with the city rather than with the country. Some cities of a hundred thousand people and more are but exaggerated country towns; they exist to serve the country districts and are kept alive by the business they do, directly or indirectly, with the people out on the farms. The country town, as it is talked of here, is the town, big or little, that does most of its business with the country and finds its prosperity in the prosperity of country people.

HOW OUR TOWNS CAME TO BE

The first settlements in America were towns. The settlers grouped themselves by the seashore or on the banks of a river into a compact little community. Before them stretched the great areas of untended land, land that was to be made into the countryside of a nation; but with all this realm most of them had at first comparatively little to do. Their business was with the lands across the sea; they had their eyes turned seaward and were commercial rather than agricultural settlements.

It was but a little while until this began to change. Plymouth was a farming community almost from the landing there; Jamestown from force of necessity soon became one. The settlers began clearing land and cultivating it. More and more they turned their eyes away from the sea and trade to the land and production. Differentiation between the farmer and the non-farmer soon grew; and more and more the men who were not themselves farmers found themselves becoming business agents of the pioneers who were pushing out beyond the village limits to develop the agriculture of America. At Jamestown, Captain John Smith was early insisting that the men get out and till the soil, and that there was hope for the infant settlement in nothing else. He saw the future of Virginia in agriculture, and though this agriculture was primarily a trading agriculture—tobacco first, other things after, if at all—it was a real agriculture. It was not long until the Virginia towns were but way stations to, and conveniences for, the plantations of the pioneer planters.

So the Quakers went out from the broad squares of the City of Brotherly Love, and so, to a greater or less extent, the countryside and country life developed from the little seaboard settlements and the trading posts farther inland.

The later settlement of the land was almost purely

an agricultural settlement. Traders, it is true, scattered themselves out through the woods and along the lakes and rivers; but the country was filled up, and the character of the new realm established, by the men who went out to possess the land. The real settler was a man who moved a little way from his neighbors to clear a patch of ground, to build a cabin, to plant corn and beans and raise his own living. The French gave way before the English largely because the early English comers had more of the land hunger and less of the commercial instinct—they were looking more for a place to live, less for an opportunity to trade.

Like a rising tide, wave after wave, these home-seekers and homemakers spread out over the continent—through the Eastern forests, across the Appalachian barrier, into the fertile valleys of the Ohio, out to the broad prairies, to be checked, but not stopped, by the arid reaches of the desert country, to surmount even the ramparts of the Rockies and to flood the plains of the Columbia and the Sacramento.

The settlement of the Eastern United States, especially, once the foothold of the white man was assured, was an agricultural settlement. The typical pioneer was the farmer who took his family and his belongings into the wilderness to make a home. Emerson Hough in *The Covered Wagon* has vividly illustrated the difference in the last great Western movement between the pioneer who put his faith in the soil and the plow—the agricultural pioneer—and the pioneer who went adventuring to find gold—the exploiter, the would-be conqueror, whether of man or nature, who sought a short-cut to fortune. The men of the latter class were heroic figures often; but the foundations of America were laid by the men who cleared the "new-grounds" or broke the first furrows through the prairie sod.

In this great building of a new empire of agriculture, the town was a subsidiary development; a secondary phase, born out of necessity rather than out of a conscious plan.

Even those pioneers who felt themselves crowded when the neighbors began to clear fields on two sides of their own were not altogether sufficient to themselves. It was possible for them to live apart from other people, but it was not altogether convenient. Such self-sufficiency made life unduly hard; in fact, more than a bit precarious. Places for getting together were needed by all, and the establishment of certain activities at certain definite sites was demanded as soon as the beginnings of settlement had been made. The mill, the blacksmith shop, the trading place—these were carried out into the new country on the very first wave of settlement. They were necessary enterprises calling for distinct types of activity. The miller found a good site by a suitable stream; it was to the convenience of the whole neighborhood that the blacksmith put his shop close by; and if the neighborhood store could be somewhere near, it was so much the better for all concerned. The beginnings of town life for that rural community had been made when these industries had been established; when some man possibly became only a half-time farmer and gave the rest of his time to grinding corn, or to shoeing horses for his neighbors, or to selling goods to them. Or another man might begin it by putting up a house with an extra room or two and taking in for the night the travelers who came that way. Or still another, a professional brother of Ichabod Crane, might begin it by bringing the children of the district together to learn their letters and by helping the preacher to secure a place in which to tell the settlers about faith and righteousness and judgment to come.

Even those pioneer farmers, of course, were town-bred men in a way; they belonged to a race which had been made up of townsmen as well as farmers for many centuries; but the thing to remember is, that once the pioneer heart was turned from the sea and the lands that lay beyond it—turned, that is, from visions of wealth through discovery or trade—to the dream of a land of productive fields enriched with herds and flocks, the settlement of America became an agricultural rather than a commercial settlement. The beginnings of the real America were made in the corn patch rather than in the trading post.

Most of the towns of this land developed out of the needs of the farmers who were scattered out over the land, and existed primarily to serve those farmer needs. Most of them exist still for the same purpose. The town was not a separate development or a separate interest; it was but a part of the community's agricultural growth, and it was a very necessary part. The early townsmen were the men able, because of special knowledge or skill or financial ability, to serve their fellow settlers in some special way.

It is true that in some of the later phases of settlement and development the town builder went right along with the farmer and helped take possession of the land. In some cases he actually went ahead—the homesteader finding fine towns laid off on the virgin prairie and nice lots all ready for him to buy when he turned off the beaten trail to break a wagon track to his particular claim. Some of the towns so laid off became established, and grew, and are towns or cities today. Others failed to live up to the hopes of their promoters and became farming lands, the long rows of corn sprouting and the billows of wheat bending where streets and squares and stately buildings had been hoped for. This sort of town building, of course, was conscious and definitely planned, but it was also artificial and unnatural, and sometimes it was largely predatory. It had in it much of essential insincerity, and much of gullible incomprehension; but still it was based on a recognition of the primary fact that where the country is, the town is called for, and that as the country develops towns will be nourished and provided for.

THE TOWN IS A COUNTRY AGENCY

The town, then, is of the country. It is country born and country nourished. Towns grow out of the farming districts as trees grow out of the soil. They grip the land and draw their sustenance from it.

Every supporting fiber of them is country-made; whatever foliage or blossom of beauty they wear is country fed.

It is recognition of this fact that is needed, recognition by both town and country. Most town folks, it is to be feared, flatly disbelieve that it is a fact. Most country folks, it is almost certain, have never thought of it. Even in the little towns—the towns from whose central squares one can catch glimpses of fields and woods — there are people who feel that the town is sufficient unto itself; at least, that its closest kinship is with the cities it aspires to be like, and not with the country about it. Out on the farms there are people, and numbers of them, who look on the town as a sort of alien growth, a parasitic growth, perhaps, or one overshadowing. The town does not see in the country its own source of being and means of life; the country does not see in the town its own fruitage of effort, its own center of interest and activity.

Townsmen who have done business with countrymen all their adult lives, countrymen who have regularly turned to town since they were children to have their wants supplied, will look on these assertions as flights of unrestrained fancy, on the comparisons drawn as a mere playing with words. Yet the man who thinks seriously for a little, who reasons honestly from cause to effect and from effect back to cause, who delves down a little into the underlying facts of town and country relationship, will soon see that they are but sober statements of demonstrable fact. The more he looks into the matter, the less doubt he will have about it, and the more clearly he will see that the relationship of the country to the town is even closer than that of the soil to the tree, that it is even as that of the mother to her child.

THE TOWN DEPENDS ON THE COUNTRY

The town not only grows out of the country; it continues to live upon the country. The town is not only the child of the country, it remains an infant in the country's arms to be nourished at the country's breasts. Only the town whose chief interests are with other lands and other people than the lands and people about it grows away from the necessity of the maternal nourishment and becomes able justly to think of itself as of equal strength with the countryside. And the number of these towns and cities is much smaller than we might without investigation suspect.

Let the farmers be prosperous, and the country town is prosperous. Let the farmers know the pinch of hard times, and hard times quickly creep into the stores and banks and shops and homes of the town and begin gripping the folks who live and do business there. Two streams flow steadily from the land into the centers of population. One of these streams is a stream of people, the country-born who go to town to become the future leaders of the town or its future drudges. The other stream is a stream of wealth, the tribute the town collects yearly and daily for services performed. Without these two life-giving streams the town would perish. Out in the fields is where things are produced; in the centers of life and commerce and industry they are traded in, and transformed, and ultimately consumed.

. This is another fact from which recognition is too often withheld. There can be found hard-headed and successful business men in any number who would instantly and eagerly deny it. It is to be doubted if the majority of townspeople—though an hour's study of statistics would tell them about it—ever realize their full dependence on the country. They think of their town as an entity, as self-supporting, never seeing that it is absolutely dependent, that it is, indeed, but a growth out of and a development from the country they so often think of as backward and stupid and wretchedly poor.

It is not surprising, perhaps, that this point of view is taken by the masses of people who have had little occasion to think of the matter; but it is surprising to see it taken by men of ability who have been in business for years, and have been for all those years drawing from the countryside wealth and comfort and social standing and many another desirable thing which many a contributing countryman has lacked.

The town is the child, the nursing child, of the country. This means that the country town merchant is interested, first of all, in the ability of country people to buy goods; that the banker is interested, first of all, in the ability of the farmers of his town's trade area to make a profit from their farming. Not all the merchant's customers, even in the very small town, are farmers; most of them in towns of size may not be. The greater part of the banker's deposits may come from his fellow townsmen, and most of his loans may be made to them. But let the crops fail, or the prices of farm products drop unduly, and what happens? The merchant knows that the purchasing power of his town customers will be reduced; the banker knows that the deposits of his town patrons will speedily decrease.

True it is that the nation has lately known some five or six years of prosperity along with a general depression of agriculture, and this phenomenon has led some financiers and economists to ask whether the time has not come when the prosperity of the farmers is no longer essential to the making of general "good times." Without attempting to make any detailed or conclusive answer to this question, two facts may be pointed out here as indicating the answer. One is, that the farmer, in common with other citizens, has been able these last few years to extend his buying considerably beyond his net income. The other is, that the towns of the farming sections have been pinched by the squeezing of their farmer neighbors. Men on the spot tell us that the bankers and merchants of Iowa towns were even more insistent on "farm relief" measures than were the farmers themselves.

For the business man of the country town, at least, the well-being of the farmer remains a prime consideration; yet sometimes this business man forgets that this is so. In one of the cities of the Central South a newspaper man was trying to interest the head of a thoroughly city-minded bank in a movement for agricultural advancement.

"I am not interested in farmers," said the banker. "Our farmer business does not amount to anything."

"Who is your largest depositor?" asked the newspaper man.

"The International Harvester Company," said the banker.

That man was just two removes from the farmer, and could not see him at all. He could see the great Chicago corporation that poured money into his vaults; but his vision did not extend to the farmers who made the corporation's deposits possible.

Two removes from the farmer, there might have been some excuse for this man's visioning of the farming districts as places from which some folks make profits and as nothing more than that; but what shall be said of the man who is next neighbor to the farmer and still sees nothing more than the banker saw in the prosperity of the country districts?

Short-sighted such a man certainly is; and to this same class of the extremely myopic belongs every town business man who thinks that his interest in country dwellers ends when he has secured from them the most money and the largest profits he can manage to get.

Chapter II

THE COUNTRY ABOUT THE TOWN

THE TOWN HELPS MAKE THE COUNTRY

The country made the town; it supports the town and keeps it alive. Also, the town helps make the country. From the town the country gets much that is essential to its welfare, much that it could not supply for itself. The country made the town, but made it to meet a country necessity. A prosperous and progressive town is a necessary accompaniment to the right sort of agricultural community. If the prosperity of the town is dependent on that of the country, it is also true, though to a slightly smaller degree, that the prosperity of the country is dependent upon the success of the town. In some ways this dependence of the country on the town increases all the time, too, as the number of people off the farm becomes relatively greater than the number on the farm, and the farmer's life becomes more like that of the modern townsman and less like that of the farmer of an earlier generation.

If it be true that the merchant in the country town must look to farmer customers to keep his business going, and that his sales rise and fall with the ability of farm folks to buy; that the country town banker draws most of his deposits, primarily or secondarily, from the productive activities of the farms of his section, and makes most of his loans

[14]

for purposes vitally connected with agriculture and country life; that the doctor, the baker, the movie manager, and the garage man must have a prosperous countryside to insure their continued prosperity and progress; it is also true that the welfare of the farmers about the town is largely proportioned to the enterprise and the acumen and the business capacity of the men who do business in that town. When the farmers prosper, the merchant sells more goods; if the merchant is the type of merchant who can buy to advantage and draw trade to his doors, the farmers and their wives get better bargains when they go to buy and so make their money do them more good. The deposits in the bank increase with the profits from the farmers' crops; the ability of the farmers to make profitable their farming increases with an increasing understanding and breadth of view on the part of the banker. No one class of citizens was for a long time more active and more potent in holding Southern farming to the old-one-crop, time-purchase, crop-lien system of farming than was that class of bankers who desired immediate big profits rather than an increasing volume of business and who insisted on the planting of cotton and yet more cotton by the men for whom they advanced money. On the other hand, the more forward-looking and far-visioned bankers of the section, who have seen the advantage of year-round farming and steady returns, have been among the most effective of all workers for a better agriculture and better conditions of life on the farm.

As with the merchant and the banker, so with "the auto-mender and the baker, the movie man and the false-tooth maker." They are all in a position, positively, to help the farmers do better and live better, or, negatively, to hinder the efforts of the countryside to advance.

THE TOWN AS A COUNTRY BUILDER

Let us particularize a little and see some of the ways in which a town, consciously or unconsciously may help to build up the country about it.

I know a country town that has developed in twenty years from an exceedingly shabby little village with mud streets and a decidedly provincial outlook to one of the leading towns of its size, measured by the business it does or by the appearance of the town itself, of the whole Southeastern section. The farming country about it has developed with it. Rather, it has developed from it; for the motive force of development came from the town more than from the country. Looking back over its last quarter century, it seems to me that the beginnings of the whole great change are to be found in three things done for itself by the town or for themselves by certain citizens of the town.

For one thing, the town decided to build streets for itself and good roads out into the country about. It literally "put over" on the country districts of the little county a bond issue to build roads. The town streets were built at an unnecessary cost, I have been told; I know that the money for the country roads was not wisely expended and that the county got less returns than it should have had for its road money. But when that road construction began there was immediately a demand for labor at better wages than had been the rule and a demand for many farm products at better prices than had been the rule. The completion of the roads brought into the county good farmers and townsmen of means from other counties. The townsmen found it easier to get out into the country, and the countrymen found themselves closer to town and better able to profit by its advantages. The number of children going from the farms about to the town high school at once increased. It was easier for them to get there, and the money with which to pay their tuition seemed easier to come by. The county so evidently profited by its road-building experience that it has been a leader in this work ever since.

Somewhere along about that same time a little group of townsmen decided to put up a poultry packing and cold storage plant. The sale of poultry had long been one of the county's main sources of cash income, but the importance of the industry had not been recognized. The poultry and eggs had been bought by two or three local dealers whose idea was to buy at the lowest possible price and who, each handling a comparatively small amount, were unable to market to best advantage. With the erection of the new plant there was an almost immediate advance in prices. Chickens and eggs came from other towns; there began to be sent to the big cities carload after carload. Out on the farms more interest was taken in poultry production because there were bigger profits in it than there had been, and also because the importance of the industry was better appreciated. The town is still a poultry marketing town, and the country about it is still a poultry producing country. The town largely developed the industry for the country.

It may have been a little before this, or it may have been a little after, that two or three merchants of the town looked about them a bit and decided that they could do a wholesale grocery business, supplying the smaller towns and the outlying country round about. It seemed to many an impractical proposal, since these merchants had to meet the competition of much larger towns nearby. But they succeeded in putting the thing over. Now this town of 5,000 people does a large wholesale business in groceries, dry goods, hardware, and other commodities.

Anyone can see how the building of the cold storage plant and the development of a better poultry market would help the farmers of the section; but the benefits those farmers would derive from the establishment of a wholesale market by the town may not be so obvious. Still, I am sure, the countrymen benefited largely by this development. With the building up of the business the town's trading territory was greatly increased in area. The merchants did more business and made more money. The town acquired a broader outlook; it had not only to consider the interests of the farmers who came to town to trade, but, as well, that of all the other little towns to which it sold goods. The prosperity of the town and its new aggressiveness meant more for the people on the farms about it, a new pride in it, new points of contact with it. Most of the benefits the country people derived from the wholesale stores in the town were indirect benefits, but they were none the less real. Farming in that county became a better occupation because those few merchants in a vision of increased business caught the gleam of an out-of-town trade and had the courage to follow the gleam.

THE FARMER'S MARKET PLACE

The town is not only the place to which the farmer goes to buy; it is also the place to which he goes to sell his products. It exists to help him pass his products on to the consumers of them as well as to supply him with the commodities and the services he can not get on the farm.

Wealth flows, as I have said, from the country to the town—flows all the time, and, in my opinion, has been flowing faster in this country than justice would demand or safety allow; but there is also a reverse flow. The farmer is all the time getting money out of the town. In fact, the most he gets comes out of the town, or through it. He has a direct and vital interest in having his town just as good a market as may be. When the labor of the town is employed at good wages and the employers of the town are making good profits, he can usually sell what he has to sell at prices that are fairly satisfactory.   The development of a new industry in town means a better market for him. To many farming districts the best thing that could happen would be the opening of a mill, or a shop, or some sort of productive and labor-employing industry in a nearby town. The farmer who can view with equanimity the shutting down of factories in his trading town, or the emptying of its dwelling houses, is a very short-sighted farmer. For he owes more than he has realized to the dwellers in those houses and the workers in those factories. Even though his products may be staples that go into the channels of world commerce, he has an interest in the prosperity of his own town, in its development as a consuming center. He can hope for the most profit from his farming only when the town is thrifty and busy and has a vigorous appetite. The banker and the merchant and the movie man and the rest of them are not only people who take a toll from him; they are as well people from whom he is in position to exact a toll. Agriculture, says Herbert Hoover, is often a better town builder than is industry. Conversely, industrial development often means more to the farmers about a town than does any local agricultural development that can take place.

THE TOWN IS A CENTER OF COUNTRY ACTIVITY

Nor is the town the countryman's market place only. It is also the center of his business activities and his intellectual life. It is this, even though he may grind his grain at a wayside mill, send his children to a school in the corner of a field, attend a

country church, and do most of his trading at a
cross-roads store. The town is still the place to which
he must turn for many things, from which he must
wait for the coming of many others. It is his local
seat of government; from it come his newspapers
and his contact with the outside world; the things he
buys and sells come and go through it; the social
customs and ideas of his neighborhood are modeled
more or less closely on the customs and ideas of the
nearest town of importance. Usually, when he wishes
to see a man not of his immediate neighborhood, or
get in touch with an activity not strictly local, he
goes to town. Even if he wishes only to get a new
idea or to get a new thrill, he turns, as a rule, to the
town—to the place where the friendly politicians
and the wise editors, the learned professors and the
eloquent preachers congregate. Many towns are in-
tellectually poor, as many are materially poor; but
still, intellectuality along with wealth tends to flow
townwards and to settle there.   The more progressive and business-like the farmer is, as a general rule,
the closer his connections with, the better his understanding of, the freer his dealings with, the town.

Most farmers' clubs, even, and country organizations of all kinds, when they pass the stage of strictly
local interests and activities, find themselves meeting
in town and looking to the town for a dozen helps
and conveniences and opportunities they can not find
out in the country. The country town is the organized and specialized part of the country, its place of
business, its connecting link with the world of men.

THE HEART OF THE COUNTRYSIDE

Using another figure, the town is the heart of the countryside, the vital center through which the life currents flow, a steady stream of wealth and labor and interest and manifold activity flowing into it to keep it alive and at work, another stream flowing out of it to vitalize and quicken and renew and gladden the very extremities of its tributary farming districts.

This the town is and has been, inevitably, but almost unconsciously, through all the years. This is what it should be, consciously, purposely, much more completely and effectively in the years to come. And because it is the very heart of his economic and his social organism, the countrymen should have a direct and abiding interest in it and its welfare. When he concludes that it is a thing foreign to him, or a parasite preying upon him, and that his interests are entirely distinct from, or even opposed to its interests, he is making a mistake second only in magnitude and importance to the error of the townsman who fancies that he and his fellow citizens of the town are sufficient unto themselves and that the country exists only to contribute to their prosperity and satisfaction.

Chapter III

THREE TOWN AND COUNTRY PARABLES

THE TOWN THAT FOUND ITS FUTURE

There is a certain town in the dark tobacco district that had lived and grown and to some extent prospered by the tobacco crops the farmers of that county grew. It had become a town of seven or eight thousand people, and the handling of tobacco was its main business. The main occupation of the farmers about it was the growing of tobacco. These farmers, too, lived and increased in number as time went on, and prospered to a certain degree. That degree was not a very intensive one, however—a few of them made considerable money; most of them made very little money; some of them made no money at all, but grew poorer and poorer as the years went by. On the whole, they did not do as well as the people of the town. There was more profit accruing from the buying and re-selling, the handling and warehousing of the tobacco, than there was from the raising of it. Some few men in the town made a lot of money out of these activities. But the average business man of the town did not make so much money. He had good years and bad years, these years running well along with the good years and bad years of the tobacco growers. He found a profit—in good years a big profit—in supplying the tobacco growers with what they had to eat and wear while they were growing

their tobacco crops; but occasionally there would
come a year when tobacco did not sell for enough
to pay for the cost of growing it, and then he would
have a season of loss. In such seasons the merchants
of the town would find themselves with many bad
bills, and the banks, having many notes they could
not collect, would have to make forced sales sometimes and do a generally decreased and uncertain
business.

There was a general feeling against the town out
in the country. The farmers felt that the townsmen
were getting the better of them, and did not hesitate
to say so. They, or many of them at least, denounced
the warehousers and the bankers and the supply merchants along with the "tobacco trust" and the "specu-
lators." The more outspoken and extreme tobacco
growers did not hesitate to say that they were robbed
by the men in town, and unquestionably believed it.

To this county came an energetic young farm
agent. He looked over the situation and saw that
something was wrong—not something only, but a
number of things. The farming system was wrong,
for one thing; the farmers of the county were not
making as much money as they should have been
making for the amount of work they did or the
amount of land they tended. The business of the town
was not what it should have been in a county of such
natural resources and so many people. The town's
business policy had been wrong; it had been trying
to get as much as possible out of a set of consumers
with small incomes, and had seemingly never thought

of trying to increase those incomes and so provide
itself with a larger source of supply. The feeling of
the country people toward the town was wrong; but
so was the feeling of the town people toward the
country. The one thought of the other as a parasite;
the other was actually, though perhaps unconsciously,
trying to be, in part at least, a parasite—it was trying to get more than fair pay for the services rendered, more than its share of the wealth the country
was producing.

So the county agent got to work. He began by
trying to show the farmers a better way of farming,
by trying to teach them to be less dependent upon a
single crop for their income, by being less dependent
upon what they had to buy for a living. He talked
gardens, and chickens and hogs; he interested some
of them in sheep or in dairy cows. He sought to have
them grow tobacco as a surplus crop instead of making it their sole source of support. And while he was
trying to interest the farmers in these new activities
and this new ideal of farming, he was trying with
equal zeal to interest the business men of the town.
He preached the same doctrine to banker and merchant and professional men that he preached to tobacco growers, telling them that what was good for
the producer out on the farms must ultimately be
good for them. He made them see it, too—the men in
the town as well as the men in the country; and having made them see that their interests were essentially
the same, he had little trouble in bringing them together to work for a common end, the agricultural
and business development of the country.

Every year in that county there are community
picnics in mid-summer, town folks and country folks
meeting together in a social way. Along with these
social meetings there is a county-wide leaders' conference at which representatives from the farms and
the town meet together and plan the work of agricultural development for the coming year. This program, once worked out, is put through as a matter
of course. The county court expects to appropriate
the money asked for the work. If extra money is
needed for some new line or some unusual development, the agent and the farmers expect the business
men to help get it, and the business men expect the
same thing. The solidarity of the town and country
has been so emphasized, and so realized, that the old
feeling of hostility on the one side and of indifference
and superiority on the other side has almost passed
away. The work of that first county agent was so productive of results that it made him a marked man
and brought him an early promotion. Another agent
carries on the work along the same general lines. The
progress of the county the last half-dozen years, despite the general depression the dark tobacco business
has known, has been greater than in any equal period
in its history. It has acquired a new faith in itself and
a new confidence in the future, and has become filled
with new dreams and new ideals. All over the land
the story of its achievements has been told. There
would have been no such story to tell if the men in
that country town had not been able to grasp the
fact that the welfare of the farmer was their welfare,

and that in working for his prosperity they were but helping themselves to prosper.

This is a true story. It is also a parable; a parable for all the country towns that have not yet found their future in the country about them.

THE STORY OF A COUNTRY BANKER

"Hear another parable"—the parable of a country town banker who realized late in life the relationship of his business and of himself to the farmers and the farming of his county. This, too, is a true story:

This banker lives in a farming county of the lower South. He is distinctly "the" banker of the county. Other bankers live and do business there, but this man is the head of the county's largest bank and is the county's financial authority. What he says about financial affairs is likely to go in that part of the country.

When the cotton growers of his state began the organization of a co-operative marketing association this man flatly disapproved of the idea. He said right out that it was not the proper thing, that the farmer's business was to grow things, and that when the cotton was grown it should be sold to the dealers. Most important of all, he said that he had not one cent to lend to cotton growers who wished to finance the marketing of their crop; that the holding back of the crop, or part of it, from the markets was speculation, and that it was bad business for farmers to speculate.

The farmers, or some of them, organized, becoming members of the State Cotton Growers Association and selling cotton through it; but they found it hard to get the money they needed to carry the cotton past the regular selling time, and they found the process of organization a slow and difficult one. Men in that county had confidence in that banker's financial acumen. They were a bit wary of a project that he so positively disapproved of and discredited.

One day there came into that town a farmer from another part of the state. He came as a representative of the State Cotton Growers Association. His business was not with the cotton growers of that county, but with that particular banker. He told the banker plainly and frankly that he had come to see him, that he had three or four days to spend in the town, and that at the banker's convenience he wished to present the organized farmers' side of the question and to tell a few of the things cotton growers have to consider and to deal with. The banker agreed to listen, and the two men had a series of talks drawn out through three or four days. The talks were brief at first, for the banker was a busy man; but they became longer as the days went on, for he began to be interested and to see some things in a new light.

The farmer began by saying that the purpose of a co-operative marketing association is not to hold cotton off the market for a speculative rise in price, but to market it in an orderly fashion as the market demands it. The rush of cotton to the markets in the fall faster than the manufacturers can consume it inevitably depresses the price below what it ought to

be; for the men who buy it must buy it on a speculative basis. They know they will have to hold it, or
a good part of it, for several months, and they must
buy it at a price that will make holding safe. The increases in cotton prices that come with almost every
recurring spring profit the growers of cotton very
little—the poorer growers practically nothing at all.
They have long since sold their cotton. The farmers'
organization holding cotton for gradual marketing
must assume the risk the cotton buyer takes; but
organized farmers can take this risk, can carry the
cotton over to the time it is needed, as cheaply as
any one else; and the fact that the buyers stay in the
business and usually accumulate much more money
than do most of the growers is a pretty good indi-
cation that it does pay to sell cotton at intervals
throughout the year rather than to crowd it all on
the market in two or three months. In a word, the
banker was told that if the farmers should market
their cotton in an orderly manner and in accordance
with market demands they would get more money for
it than they would get by selling it as soon as ginned
to meet obligations they have incurred to produce it.

The banker could see the point of this. He knew
it to be true; knew that if the farmers could hold
their cotton and let it out gradually they would get
more for it.

Then the farmer went on to say that the average
cotton grower is not very well paid for his work.
The profits of the men who actually grow the cotton
—taking them one year with another—are very small

indeed. "Cotton cropper" and "poor man" are almost synonymous terms in the cotton country.

The banker knew these things. There could be no question about them.

Then the farmer went on to point out to the banker that, after all, the prosperity of a bank must be limited by the prosperity of the people who do business with it, and that any extra profit that might come to the farmers of an agricultural county would be bound to bring some extra profits to the banks of that county. The more depositors a bank has, the more money it will have to do business with; the more prosperous the borrowers are, the more they will borrow and the safer the loans will be. Bankers in the cotton country sometimes get big profits from foreclosures, and sometimes they are able to lend money at rates that have no relationship with the statutes on interest; but foreclosures are not desirable features of legitimate banking business, and the man who needs money so badly that he is willing to pay an exorbitant price for it is usually a man whose ability to pay back is so uncertain that the high rate barely compensates for the risk taken. The banker knew all this, once he came to think of it—knew that it would be better for him to do business with farmers who were getting ahead, who had money to deposit and who would likely meet their obligations promptly, than to do business with men whose farming was on a very narrow margin of profit, and consequently on a very narrow margin of security. He might be able to drive harder bargains with farmers of the latter class; but he could make more money in a term of years by doing business with men of the former class. The man who had the ability to become the financial dictator, almost, of his county did not have to be argued into seeing that the prosperity of the county was inevitably linked up with his own prosperity and that of his bank.

It remained for the farmer to convince the banker that the farmers' plan of organized marketing was a sound and practical one. He did it, but that part of it need not concern us here. The point is that when he was through the banker had voluntarily pledged himself to further the organization of the cotton growers and to see to it that the association of that county had all the money it might need.

The banker simply needed to get the country viewpoint, to realize truly his position in the county, his relationship with the farmers of the county and his duty to them. He had failed, strangely it may seem, but just as many small town business men fail, to see that his business was a real part of the farming business of his community, and that when he tried to run it as a business entirely independent of the men who were his ultimate customers he was lessening its usefulness and curtailing his own chances to make money. The lesson of the story, if it has one —and it seems to me that it has—is not that bankers should support the co-operative movement, but that they should "take thought for the morrow" by taking thought for the welfare of the agriculture of their communities.

L and C are two towns of nearly the same size, in the same state, county seats of counties with about the same population. Both towns own hydro-electric lighting and power plants. L's plant has been in operation much the longer, dating from 1908. The C plant began operation the first of 1922. Rates for electric current are low in both towns, L having a rate of 10 cents per kilowatt hour for light and 4 cents for power, while C asks only 7 cents for light and 2 cents for power.

The L power plant is on a little stream running close by the town; the plant was built by a bond issue, of course, and bonds have been issued since to enlarge the plant and to rebuild it—or rather, to build a new plant to take the place of the one the town had outgrown. All the power available is being used now, and the demand for electric service is such that in dry seasons the "load" is greater than the plant can bear. In both 1924 and 1925 some of the users of power were cut off for a time.

The C plant is a pretty bit of engineering enterprise, a hill having been tunneled through to enable the waters of a picturesque stream—Falling Water, its appropriate and charming name—to be put to work for the town. Only about half the available power is demanded by the town, or used.

Both investments have been profitable; L, especially, has made a success of its plant, making it meet most of the town's expenses these latter years. The hydro-electric plant has paved the streets of the town, helped keep its schools going, held taxes down to a very low figure. One of the great electric corporations has, since this was first written, offered for it more than twice as much as the town has in it. As stated, the demand for service has increased with, even faster than, the ability of the plant to supply it. If the plant is finally sold, as many citizens are coming to think it should be, it will be simply because of the fact that it is no longer adequate to meet the town's need, and because of the increasing realization that an electric service from a widely distributed and interlocking combination of service units is much more flexible and dependable than service from a single unit can be. The town's people are inclined to boast about their power plant.

The people of the other town like to talk about the low cost of electricity in the town—"The lowest in all the state," one man told me and probably he was right.

Despite the lower cost of service in C, however, the use of electricity has increased much more rapidly in L these last few years. At the second of two visits I made to C three years apart, I was told that the plant was still using only half the power available, and that the greater part of what increase there had been in the consumption of current was due to the increased use by the city itself for street lighting and so on. C still has current for sale; half of the power of its splashing stream is still unutilized.

The two towns have pursued very different policies.

C steadfastly refuses to sell power outside of the town. The farmer living just beyond the town limits can not get his home lighted or his water pumped by the town's hydro-electric plant. The town authorities have not thought of that farmer as a part of the town's business population, or as a contributor to its development; they have not thought of developing the town by helping the farming country about it to develop. Instead they have been trying to develop it by getting new industries—factories, etc.—to locate in it, and have been trusting to their cheap power to bring those industries. It takes something more than cheap power, however, to bring new industries to a town these days, and the industrial development of the town lags.

On the other hand, L has tried to increase the use of electricity by supplying electric fixtures to the users of current at just about the actual cost of delivery or installation. It has run lines out into the surrounding country in all directions as farmers wished for service. One little village seven miles away is supplied with current. The net profit from this village runs about $200 a month. The country lines pay a profit, too; and the farmers profit by having them. Town and county develop together, and the county is generally spoken of as having led the state in progress these latter years. Business men there have no doubt as to whether it pays a town to consider the county about it, or as to whether town and county are part of each other. They have profited by not doubting; C has almost surely lost money by lacking faith in its countryside.

THE LESSON OF THE PARABLES

Other stories might be told; stories of other towns that have found their future in the greater prosperity and the finer development of the country about them; stories of other townsmen who have come to see that the well-being of their business, if it is to be permanent, must rest on the foundation of a progressive and profit-producing agriculture. To tell a long list of such stories would be useless. These have been told only to substantiate the statements made, to make plain the facts asserted in the first chapter, to show just how the country nourishes the town and how the town, in return, may and should labor with and for the country.

Mutuality of the interests of country town and countryside is not a fancy or a theory but a demonstrable fact. It must be accepted as a fact and made the basis of any program of town building before that program can be made at all comprehensive and before it can be carried through to any satisfactory conclusion.

Chapter IV

CONFLICTING INTERESTS OF TOWN AND COUNTRY

THE BATTLE BETWEEN BUYER AND SELLER

The country town and the farming districts about the town have many interests in common; but not all the interests of town and country are identical. There is conflict between the man in town and the man in the country, conflict immemorial and inevitable. If the town is to find its rightful place in the scheme of rural life, it is just as essential that this conflict be recognized as that the value and the necessity of town and country co-operation be recognized.

When the town is a seller, the country, as a general rule, is a buyer. What the country has to sell, the town buys. Always and everywhere, the buyer's interests are opposed, to a certain extent, to those of the seller. A large margin of profit is what the seller seeks; it is for that margin that he is doing business. The lowest price is what the buyer looks for; his success as a buyer is determined by his ability to get things as cheaply as possible.

There is, of course, a limit to the real profit to be had from either skillful selling or economical buying; but no one can say just where the limit is in a given case, and one can go a long way in actual business practice before he reaches the point where it would have been better for him individually if he had got less for what he had to sell or had paid more for the thing he bought.

If the merchant in the country town, for example, has a prosperous farming community to sell to, he will do a much larger business and probably make a much larger total profit on his business than if he must do business with a poor community. It is conceivable that he could exact a margin of profit so large on the sale of necessities that he would keep his customers from buying anything except those necessities, and so sharply limit his total sales and his possible profits. There is reason to believe that this very thing has taken place over much of the cotton country, where "supply merchants" have supplied very poor cotton growers with comparatively small quantities of very cheap goods, getting a big profit on the goods sold, but never doing a large business because of the simple inability of their patrons to buy extensively. The big profits of many of these merchants have actually worked to keep them from making very much money for themselves, because those profits have been so great as to keep their only possible customers poor. One may get all the money another man has, and still have very little money for himself. If the second man has only a few dollars, he can be made quite poor without making the first man wealthy. Still, it is unquestionably better for a merchant to get a profit of 25 per cent on the goods he sells than for him to sell them at 20 per cent profit. His gains from the additional 5 per cent will certainly outweigh any advantages he might derive from the greater purchasing power his customers would have because of their saving of the 5 per cent.

On the other hand, the man who buys goods will likely be able to get better margins from a merchant who is making much money than from one who is making very little. It is to his interest also to do business with a man of means. But if he can save 5 per cent on his purchases, he is getting more for himself directly than he could reasonably hope to secure indirectly from the additional prosperity the extra 5 per cent would bring to the merchant.

When a farmer goes to the bank to borrow money it is to the interest of both farmer and banker that the farmer be making money out of his farming and that the banker have a sound institution; but when it comes to the question as to whether the farmer shall pay 6 per cent or 7 per cent for the money, there is a direct conflict of interest.

The farmer profits when the woolen mill in the town can sell its blankets, because that means that the stockholders in, and the employers of, the mill will have more money with which to buy butter and eggs and potatoes and roasting-ears. The mill owners and employees profit when the farmer can sell his truck at good prices, because that means a bigger demand for blankets. But when it comes to the direct exchange, the farmer wants to give just as few bushels of potatoes as may be for his blankets, while the mill owner or the mill hand wishes to secure his bushel of potatoes for the equivalent of the profit on

the smallest number of blankets, or the equivalent of
the fewest possible hours of labor.

So with every man doing business or performing
labor in the town. It is clearly to his interest to have
his margins or his labor count for all they can when
he goes to buy the things the farmer has to sell. With
much mutuality of interest, town and country have
also a sharp diversity, in some cases an actual conflict of interest.

THE CITYWARD FLOW OF WEALTH AND PEOPLE

Nor is this direct personal conflict between buyer
and seller the only conflict between town and country. There is another conflict that is of fundamental
importance and that has been waged for more centuries than history has recorded. Always the town
has taken from the country more than it has given
back; it has absorbed the best of the country's products without making any return that was apparently
adequate. This absorption and concentration have to
be if the town is to live and to thrive; but always
the country must struggle against them if it is not
to lose so much that it becomes poorer and poorer
and less capable of self protection.

The wealth the country produces flows into the
town in a broad, full, sweeping stream, while the re-
turning stream is, in comparison, but a rippling
brook. The country districts do not hold the wealth
they produce; the cities, even the little towns, acquire
more than they produce.

Nor is it wealth alone that flows from the country

to the town. Along the same channel goes the best youth of the country. The towns drain the country of ability and energy and ambition just as surely as they drain it of gold. A majority of the most capable young men and women of any rural section will likely be living in some town when they die. To the towns go the alert, the enterprising, the best educated. The dreamers of dreams, the seizers of opportunity, the masters of destiny are, in the mass, townward bound. Year by year they go—boys and girls fresh from school, active men and women who have come to stand in one way or another above their neighbors, retired farmers and their wives with the prestige of success about them. The country must struggle all the time to save from the town the best of its blood and its brain and its mental and spiritual brawn.

Not only is it quality of mankind of which the town robs the country. It is of mass of manhood as well. Always the country districts have a larger percentage of children in their population than have the urban districts. The people on the farms of America are raising and providing for 2,000,000 more children than are an equal number of the people in the cities. In 1920, 27.6 per cent of the urban population was under 15 years of age. Of the rural population, 36.2 per cent was under 15 years. "Rural" population here includes the people in the towns of less than 2,500 population as well as the people on the farms. The small town has in its population, as might be expected, a larger propor-tion of children than the city has, and a smaller

proportion than the farm has. The last census figures
show the following groupings by age of the urban
proportion than the farm has. The last census figures
population, the rural population, and the strictly farm

	Under 10 yrs.	10 to 20 yrs.	21 yrs. and over
Urban	19.0	18.5	62.5
Rural	24.6	23.0	52.4
Farm	25.7	24.7	49.5

The small town pays toll of its youth to the great
city, in its turn exacting a toll from the open country.

The country produces the child, cares for him
through the care-demanding days of his infancy,
feeds and clothes him through his unproductive
years, bears the expense of his education, and turns
him over to the city a finished product, at the beginning of his productive period of life. The economic
drain made by this process upon the country districts
is terrific. There seems to be no help for it. It is not
on record that any city has ever kept up its own population. Even though the proportions of farm and
town populations should be stabilized, this drain on
the farm would continue; for the age-compositions
of the two populations would undoubtedly continue
to be different.

The country town here is both a way-station on
the route from farm to city and an active recipient
of country youth. The small town loses population
to the larger city and gains it from the country.

THE COUNTY THE UNIVERSITY ROBBED

The country can afford to send some of its young people to the city; but it has been sending too many, too many especially of the ones it most needed to keep. A state university president was talking to me. He was talking about one of the most backward counties in his state, a county purely rural, isolated, with but a single town above village size. From this county two young men had gone to the university. They were young men of more than ordinary promise; one of them especially gifted and with unusually high aspirations. Neither of them was going back to the home county. They had ambitions it could not satisfy; they sought for opportunities it seemed not to hold. "I can not advise them to go back," said the president, "for there is nothing there for them. It would not be fair to ask them to do it. Still, when I think of these boys, it seems to me that I am working against that county instead of for it. I have helped to take its best away from it, to deprive it of the type of young men who would do most for it if they should stay at home. The university will have helped those boys, but it will not have helped the people back in that county."

It is a sore problem, and an old one. The best of the country youth, drawn by the very advance of civilization, goes from the farms to the county seats, on to the state metropolises, and on to New York or Chicago. So the youth of like fiber went up from the ancient farms to Rome and to Ninevah, no doubt, and to Thebes of the hundred gates. The exodus has been going on since the first towns sprang up in the midst of the fields; the problem of how to control it and keep it within bounds so that the farming country will not finally be deprived of the seed stock of its best humanity is older than any civilization of which we know; and it is a problem as yet unsolved. The immeasurable fecundity of the fields enables them to go on, age after age, producing the food and the clothing for mankind, producing wealth and men to labor; but not always have they continued to produce brain and vision. Again and again they have failed to supply the cities with the new vigor and the new vitality cities must have if they are to live, and again and again nations have gone down into the dust, weary and old and nerveless, seemingly, because the great life-currents from the fields had ceased to flow.

For the country can be drained to depletion of human as well as of material wealth. Always it must fight to hold for itself sufficient of its own best to keep itself strong and aspiring and dynamic. When the town draws too strongly on it, the power to produce the finest type of manhood seems to fail and the countryside becomes the breeding place of a peasantry, poor in goods and poor in spiritual vitality. When that has taken place, the doom of both country and city can be plainly described, a shapeless portent of darkness looming through the gray uncertainties of time.

THE WITHHELD REWARD

It is needless to ask why the wealth of the country flows to the towns; needless to ask why the children of the farms turn their steps away from the grassy paths and toward the paved streets.

It is a matter of rewards. Opportunity is in most cases a creation of mankind. Few would rather be a ragged ruler in a shepherd's hut than a silken-robed subject in Babylon.

The dollar has a better chance to gather to itself nickels and cents in the city than it has in the country. The seeker for power or for leadership, or for self-expression, has a better chance to impress himself upon his fellows where men are numerous than where they are few. The rewards for pleasing, or serving, or dominating many men are greater than for pleasing, or serving, or dominating a few.

The country loses wealth to the town, in a word, because it is easier to make money in the town than in the country; it loses its choicest sons and daughters to the town because the town offers them greater rewards than it has to give.

If the country is to attain its own possible best, it must grow towns along with its crops and contribute to the upbuilding of many activities and industries distinct from its own. The automobile makers give the rural districts such roads as those districts could never have secured for themselves, and they give the man and woman in the country a freedom of movement and a possibility of accomplishment no country people have ever brought about by their own efforts. If country people are to keep their bodies clean and their houses comfortable, there must be men to make bathtubs and electric lighting plants

and furnaces and fans. Book publishers and opera
singers and movie magnates and radio builders are
necessary contributors to the education and the
amusement of the folks back on the farm. The country can live by itself alone, but it can not live the
life of civilization.

Yet when it comes to pass that the maker of automobiles or bathtubs or furnaces can make profits
such as the farmer can not make and pay wages
such as the farmer can not pay, the grass begins to
grow in the corn and the palings to fall off the yard
fence and the porches to go unswept and the books to
remain unread. Then, in their turn, start away from
the country the farmer who has been able to lay up
more money than his fellows and the boy who is
determined to have for himself the desirable things
of life.

Up to a certain point, the growth of the towns
and the development of urban business means better
things for the farmer; beyond a certain point, every
increase in comparative wealth and comfort and
progress of the town promotes a decadence of country life. Too great opportunity in the city means lessened opportunity in the country.

Here again, it is naturally impossible to draw any
fixed line, to say definitely and specifically just what
the proportionate rewards of town and country
should be; but to any thoughtful observer it must
be obvious that in recent years in the United States
the towns have had too much to offer, comparatively
speaking, and the country too little.

It is a natural thing that urban population should increase faster than rural population; but it is almost a certainty that the cityward trend of late has been too strong for the nation's highest welfare. It is inevitable that the country retain less wealth than it produces and the towns accumulate more than they produce; but it would be hard for any fair-minded man to believe that the farmers have had fair play for their labor or fair returns on their investment this last generation, as compared with the pay for work and the returns on investment in other lines of business.

There has come of late to the rural districts a new class consciousness, a feeling of agricultural solidarity, that has surprised city dwellers and even the farmers themselves. Farmers have been thinking and feeling with and for their fellow farmers as probably never before in the nation's history. To some this seemed a portent of evil; to others it has seemed the dawning of hope. In any case, it has impressed itself upon the national consciousness and has caused even the people least connected with farming to realize that there is a country state of mind and that there are special and definite country needs.

Whatever may be said and thought of this new feeling, this disturbing impulse, it is, after all, but an effort of the country to save for itself something of what the town has been taking from it—something more of the wealth it produces, something more of promise and opportunity for its children, something more of voice and influence in the direction of the nation's political and economic policies.

When farmers assert their right to have, as a matter of course, the things that would have been impossible luxuries in the country a generation ago, they are not asserting any more than the right of country life, as we of America have known it in the past, to continue its existence and to keep up the contributions it has been making to the life of the nation. Let townsfolk not deceive themselves. If the town child goes to a good school while the country child goes to a poor school; if the town woman rides rapidly and comfortably when she goes shopping while the country woman must travel slowly and uncomfortably through the mud; if the town man takes his bath in a bathtub and has his choice of a dozen diversions in the evening while the country man washes in a pan and wonders what to do with himself before going to bed, the country is going to have an increasing feeling of resentment toward the town; and that feeling, however illogical it may be, is not going to be altogether without reason. Moreover, if the country districts are too closely drained, become too different in standards of life and in social opportunity from the town, our old tradition of great leaders coming out of humble farm homes will become in the course of a few generations but an old tradition, and our old reality of cities and towns kept fresh and vital by the influx of freshness and vitality from the country will cease to be a reality. For the stock that produces leaders, the blood that carries freshness and vitality in its currents, will not remain where life is permanently lacking in zest and opportunity. When the country struggles to keep for itself more of its own best and to bring to itself more of the best of the towns, it is but fighting for its life.

Not that there will not always be men to till the fields and produce food for the world; but that, if the town too far outstrips the country in the things that make life desirable and effort productive, there will be a steady deterioration of country stamina along with the deterioration of country finances.

Here is a conflict of immediate interest between town and country that is no less real and no less inevitable than the conflict of interest between buyer and seller. It may be a bit less obvious, but it exists just as truly as the other. Like the other, too, there is for it no ending. The only hope is that each side may be sufficiently strong in the conflict to secure for itself something like justice, sufficiently intelligent and fair-minded to understand something of the needs of the other side and to be willing to confer and to concede that justice may be done. So can the conflict be made a friendly rivalry rather than the unfriendly squabble it has at times threatened to become.

THE TOWN MAY BECOME PARASITIC

It must not be forgotten, either, that it is possible for the town to become more or less parasitic, for it to live as a selfish feeder upon the country instead of living, as it should, as an active co-worker with the country. Certain businesses in the town easily become to a greater or less degree parasitic—that is, they come to absorb wealth without really producing

wealth or contributing in any fair degree to the welfare of others. Indeed, it would not be hard to find
in any town of any size certain men and certain
business interests that could be dispensed with without any loss to the community, and with specific
gain to the majority of other individuals and to more
important interests.

Every little town, almost, has its loan shark,
its driver of hard bargains, who knows how to take
advantage of the needs of others and collect more
than a legal or an equitable rate of interest for the
use of his money. Every town has in it some man
who has grown rich from the unearned increment of
land values, a man who has held his land idle and
out of use, letting the labor and thrift of other men
make him wealthy. These men, stock examples of the
parasite, may prey upon their fellow townsmen as
well as upon the countrymen; but there are others
who draw their nourishment almost exclusively from
the veins of the agriculturist. The tobacco "pin-
hooker" is such a man, the local cotton buyer who
buys when he can do so at less than market price
simply to sell again to the real dealer, the stock trader
who buys and sells the same way. Then, of course,
there are purely fraudulent enterprises that make their
appeal especially to the countryman; and, more important than any or all of these, there are the perfectly legitimate businesses and the perfectly respectable
business men who have, by taking more than their
share, become semi-parasitic. The merchant who by
reason of monopoly or other favoring circumstance

gets more than a fair profit in his sales, or buys the farmer's produce for less than a fair price, is in this class. So is the banker who is able to charge, and does charge, the countryman more than a reasonable rate of interest; and so is the professional man who is in a position to make his services bring him more than a just reward. The tendency toward this sort of semi-parasitism is great in most towns, and it is to be feared that there is an altogether too general disposition on the part of townsmen to excuse and encourage it, to think of whatever brings wealth to the town as commendable, even though it takes that wealth from the country about the town.

As just one example of this state of mind, take the matter of rural fire insurance. Whoever heard of a town encouraging the farmers about it to organize, or to insure with, a farmers' mutual insurance company if there chanced to be even one or two "old-line" insurance agencies in the town? Yet, the savings of the mutual to the farmers, and the safety of this form of insurance, are matters established beyond question by the statistics.

Here again, there can be no fixed line drawn, no final judgment passed on any town; but it must be obvious from the way certain classes of business have thrived in disregard of the farmer's lack of prosperity, often directly at the farmer's expense, that, by some means or other, these businesses have been able to fasten themselves, leech-like, onto the farmer's pocketbook and to draw from it until it becomes en-

tirely too flat. The erroneous idea, still held by many
country folks, that the people who live in the towns
live on the farmer just as lice and mites live on his
chickens, has not been altogether without evidence
that seemed to bolster it up. An enlightened town perception will recognize both the existence of this notion and the reason for its continued existence. Such
an enlightened perception will recognize, too, the danger there is to the country, and eventually to the town
itself, in whatever business practices or conditions
make it possible for the man in town to "bleed" the
man in the country.

In the conflict of town and country interests, the
town usually has advantages which it will be wise
not to use. Not only justice, but good business policy
as well, demands that the farmer and the farm be
allowed to keep what is their own. If nothing else,
the towns will do well to keep in mind that the rela-
tive supply of countrymen to townsmen is growing
smaller all the time, and that this very fact may one
day give to the countryman certain of the advantages in the inevitable economic conflict between town
and country which the townsman now has. In the
controversies of politics, power belongs to the majorities; in the controversies of business, power usually joins itself to the minorities. More buyers and
fewer sellers give the seller more power and increase
his profits.

Chapter V

SOME MATTERS OF DISPUTE

GENERAL PRINCIPLES AND PARTICULAR POINTS

It is good to consider things from the heights of outstanding general principles; but it is also good to get down close to things and consider their particular features. One's conclusions about any matter of which he has studied only the particularities are likely to be wrong conclusions—lacking the comprehensive viewpoint, he will draw about as correct conclusions as did the "six men of Indostan" who went to view the elephant. Conversely, general principles are of little value if they can not be applied to details.

It is easy enough to say that town and country have interests in common, but before anything can be done to further those common interests there must be agreement as to what they are. It is as obvious as daylight that town and country have conflicting interests and matters of dispute, but no harmonious adjustment of any dispute need be hoped for until the attention of both parties is given to both sides of the case.

So for a little consideration of some of the matters about which town and country are still in disagreement.

WHERE SHALL THE FARMER TRADE?

Merchants in country towns do not worry as much, apparently, about what the big mail-order houses are going to do to them as they did a decade or so ago. Country town newspapers and chambers of commerce do not spend as much time as they used to spend urging the people about their towns to "Buy at Home"; but there is, in the classic language of a hill-country friend of mine, a "heaven's plenty" of both agitation and advice to be discovered yet. Not yet are we done hearing that, "When you spend a dollar at home it stays there and passes around; but when you send it away it is gone for good." Indeed, it is probable that some devoted town boosters have said this so often and with so much emphasis that they actually believe it "even unto this day." There are really people about most towns who feel that the farmer who orders from a distance goods that he could have bought at home is a sort of traitor to the town; and there are many more who think that every development of the mail-order business is bound to make life harder and profits smaller for the local merchant.

This is a matter the country town merchant needs to look at from the customer's point of view, a matter he needs to quit feeling about and begin thinking about. For the idea that the farmer is in any way duty bound to buy from his local merchant is folly pure and simple, and the idea that the mail-order houses are likely ever to put the progressive local merchant out of business is an idea born of unreasoning fear.

It is a practical certainty that in nine purchases out of ten the farmer living close to a progressive and fairly broad-minded town can do better, all things considered, buying from his local store than he can buying from a mail-order house in a distant city. It is absolutely certain, however, that there are times and occasions when the farmers can save money, or get better goods, or come nearer getting the thing he desires, by ordering it from a reliable mail-order house than by buying it at home. In such cases, and at such times, it is unmistakably the farmer's right to buy where he can get the best bargain. It is not too much to say that his duty to his family and to himself requires that he do it. For the farmer, when he goes to buy, should exercise the same right of choice, and make the same investigation as to costs and quality, that the good merchant will make when he goes to buy. It is a matter of business pure and simple. The farmer customer has a right to say, in effect, to the local merchant, "If you can not give me as good bargains as I can get elsewhere, I must buy elsewhere." When the chambers of commerce and the county papers urge the farmer to spend his money at home, they should be—and generally are—wasting their breath unless they can show him where he will profit by buying at home. The true policy of town building is that policy which would concern itself first of all with making it to the farmer's interest to do his trading with the local merchant. The spirit that would have the farmer buy from this merchant when he could get better value for his money by buying elsewhere is a spirit that considers the farmer's welfare very little. The town offering

the farmer such advice has yet too much selfishness
in its make-up and too little understanding.

The merchant himself may be excusable for dis-
playing this sort of selfishness; but what of the editor, and the banker, and the lawyer, and the other
business men of the town who forget to consider the
welfare of the country citizen in thinking of the welfare of a fellow citizen of the town?

They display all too plainly that with them the
farmer's welfare is a very secondary consideration.

The argument that the dollar spent with the town
merchant stays in the town to cheer the pockets of
others of the community, while the dollar sent to a
merchant in another town or city hies itself away
never to return, is too silly to need much refutation.
Unless the home merchant has bought his goods at
home and those goods have been made of home-
produced raw materials, the dollar, or a good part of
it, is going to leave town anyway. It is well for a
community to raise the things it can profitably raise
at home rather than to buy them from abroad; and
well also for it to make at home whatever it can
profitably make there; but in any modern community most of the dollars the members of that community pay out inevitably go abroad. The typical
country town does not produce its sugar, or its shoes,
or its clothing at home. The dollars spent for them
must be compensated for by the dollars that come in
from abroad to pay for the products of, or the services rendered by, the community. When a farmer
parts with his dollar the important question for him

is not where that dollar is going, or how long it is going to be on its way, but what he is going to get for it. If 25 cents of it can remain in the pocket of his local merchant and he can still get just as much for it as if the full 100 cents went abroad, it is manifestly to his interest to pass it on by way of the merchant rather than himself to send it at once abroad; but if he can get somewhere else for 90 cents what he would have to pay the merchant a dollar for, it is manifestly to his interest to speed the 90 cents onward and hold fast to the dime. The dime will be worth more to him in his own pocket than the quarter would be worth to him in the pocket of the merchant.

This is not an argument for buying away from home. Such argument is not needed. The growth of the great mail-order houses has shown that they fill a place in the national economy of distribution, just as the success of thousands of enterprising small town merchants the land over has shown that the local merchant is a necessary man and one able to hold his own. The plea is for a reasonable view on the part of the townsman of the farmer's inclination to buy abroad, for a full and frank and friendly recognition of his right to buy where he can get the most for his money, and for a study of the reasons why he so often finds, or thinks, it profitable to trade elsewhere than in his own town.

Once the small town merchants and the small towns themselves recognize that the farmer, just like anyone else, should buy where he can get the most for his money, and set out to deal with him on the basis of this recognition, they can get and hold more of his trade than they can ever secure by talking to him about the duty he owes to his local merchant and his town. The farmer is likely to be skeptical as to his duties along this line. He knows that much of this sort of talk is "buncombe," and knowing this, he is likely to decide that none of it is worth heeding. Let the merchant and the town say to him frankly, "We recognize that occasionally you can do better buying elsewhere than from us, but we also believe that in most cases we can give you more for your money than anyone else can give, and we are willing always to quote you prices in competition and to tell you just what we can do," and the problem of how to hold the farmer's trade for the home town will be solved. For if the local merchant can not show the farmer that in most cases the local store gives service and co-operation that can not be had from the distant concern in a big city, that merchant will never be much of a salesman and is in the wrong business. Live country merchants, who have the modern point of view and consider the welfare of their customers as well as their own present profits, go right ahead just as if there were no mail-order houses and no buying abroad. Most of the exhortations addressed to the farmers on their duty to buy at home need to be changed to exhortations on the duties of merchants to their customers and addressed to the small town merchants.

THE FARMER'S RIGHTFUL MARKET PLACE

The natural place for the farmer to buy things, then, is in his home town, and it is usually the best place. In this home town is also the natural place for him to sell things. It has been a fundamental source of trouble and misunderstanding that many times the towns have forgotten that the farmer is a seller as well as a buyer, that he must sell, as a rule, before he can buy. Townsmen have been so eager to sell to the farmer that they have often failed to think of him as a seller, or they have been so eager to buy from him to their own advantage that they have failed to inquire whether or not his marketing was sufficiently profitable to enable him to be a good buyer. When the town is worrying itself and lecturing the farmer over the question of where he buys, it ought also seriously to be considering the question of where he is to sell and to what advantage.

I remember that once when I was a boy on the farm I had a few potatoes to sell. I went to our town's one produce dealer. He offered me a price far below market quotations. I at once felt that something was wrong. Another farmer who had potatoes to sell had the same experience. We met and talked the matter over. A day or two later we found out that this dealer was supplying the grocers with potatoes out of a car he had bought in the Northwest, a car for which according to his own statement, he had paid considerably more per bushel than he would offer us. I sold my potatoes to one of the grocers at just what the dealer was asking for his and so made money by not selling to him; but I have never, in all these years, been able fully to forgive him. He could have paid me and the other local potato grower as much as he paid for the potatoes from another state and still have made money. It would have been to his interest and to the interest of the town, in the long run, for him to do it. But he did not see anything for himself in the development of local potato growing; he could not see beyond the big profits he expected to make on our few bushels of potatoes.

The inquirer will hear similar stories around many country towns, around the majority of them probably. It seems to be the exception, rather than the rule for a town to make an effort to see that the farmers about it have a good market for their products. Usually the effort is to get those products away from the producers at the lowest possible price. This is a perfectly natural effort, and an excusable one, when the purchaser is himself the consumer. It is even to some degree excusable when the purchaser expects to re-sell those products along with others of the same kind; he sees in that case an added profit in every reduction he can force in the purchasing price. But when this same effort is made with products which the town does not use, but exports, and which are the community's chief source of income, it is hard to find an excuse for the encouragement of it, or even the toleration of it, by those townsmen who are not themselves directly interested in the buying and selling of those products. Even the reasoning back of such encouragement is hard to comprehend.

Farmers have complained often of this attitude, complained bitterly and with reason. It has been a grievance that the local merchant was often unwilling to pay as much for a local product as he would have to pay for the same product brought in from abroad. It has been an equal grievance that even in sections where certain money crops are the main sources of the whole community income, the towns have helped to depress rather than to sustain prices of these crops. In the egg-producing sections it has been the policy of many store keepers who buy eggs to keep the price as low as possible, and the general sympathy of the town has seemed to be with these dealers rather than with the egg producers. Yet these eggs were sent elsewhere for consumption, and every increase in the profits of egg production or in the extent of the business in the community would mean money for the whole community. There is scarcely an inland town in all the cotton country in which the price of cotton has not, in years past, been forced down in the early buying season below a fair differential from prices in the central markets. A few buyers of cotton in each community have profited by this depression, to be sure; but the great majority of the people, the cotton growers, have lost, and the total amount of money coming into the community for the crop has been greatly lessened. In an article written lately for one of the leading reviews, I tried to make plain how and why it is to the interest of all Americans that cotton, a crop largely exported, should always sell at a fair price. If it sells at a price too small to give the producers of it American wages for their labor of production, it simply means the forcing down of the wages and the standard of living of a large group of our people to the levels of the "pauper labor of Europe," about which the politicians prate so much. And the same thing happens in a smaller way whenever a town helps to depress the price of the major product of the farms about it. A cotton town is interested first of all in the prosperity of the cotton belt; the prosperity of a few local cotton buyers is to it a very minor matter compared with this.

Yet the cotton belt towns have helped to depress cotton prices. The same story has been told many times in the peanut and tobacco sections. Grain growers and livestock producers have not, as a rule, found any great interest among the business men of their towns in the securing of a better price for these commodities. More often the sympathy of most of the townsmen has seemed to be with the few dealers who could profit by keeping local prices down.

Yet these same townsmen in these same towns all over the country have, at these same times, been urging the farmers to buy at home and so help promote the prosperity of the community through the prosperity of the local merchant!

No town can justly claim to be doing its full duty by the farming country about it until it makes a real effort to provide that farming country with a market for what it has to sell, until it uses its influence to help secure a fair price for the products of the farms.

The country town merchant who would have the farmers buy from him should be a willing buyer from the farmers of what they have to sell locally, and should be a willing helper in any efforts they may make to get good prices for what they sell elsewhere.

This does not mean that the merchant at the farmer's town is under any obligation to buy something for which there is no demand simply because some farmer took a notion to raise it. It does mean that when the farmers raise something for which there is somewhere a demand it is to the interest of the men whose customers the farmers are, and of the towns the farmers support, to help put those farmers in touch with the best markets and to assist them in selling their product to the best advantage.

MAKING A MARKET FOR THE COUNTRYMAN

Hear another story:

In a little country town in the hill country lives a merchant who had been buying and shipping eggs and poultry for a long time. He woke up one day to the fact that the poultry and eggs going from his town were of very poor quality and brought very low prices when they got to New York. He saw that his people were not making much profit on their chickens and that, therefore, those chickens were not adding much to the community wealth—not even adding what they should to his own wealth. He decided that better chickens would mean more money for all concerned. So he arranged to buy settings of eggs of one of the American standard breeds and agreed to supply those eggs at cost to any of his customers, letting them pay him in the fall, with one of the pullets raised from the eggs, if they preferred to pay in that way. From all around chicken raisers came to take advantage of the liberal offer. Fall came, and when his pullets came in he sold them back to the poultry raisers and found that he had made a good profit on his investment. The good flocks started in the neighborhood set people generally to talking poultry and to getting better poultry and to taking better care of their poultry. Soon he was sending out graded eggs of uniform quality and getting much better prices for them, and soon the poultry of that section was bringing a much better price because it was better poultry. With a bigger business and better prices, he found himself, naturally, making more money from his poultry business; but that was not all—his customers were making more money, too, and they had more money with which to buy other things, so that his business was a bigger thing all around. Just as these pages were being revised I saw a letter from the poultry leader of a neighboring state's farm extension work telling how the effects of this man's work had crossed the state line and were there plainly perceptible. And all this came about just because he realized that it was poor business for his county to be shipping eggs that brought less than Western eggs in New York when it could be producing just as good eggs and just as good chickens as the West produced.

Many merchants and many bankers in many towns

have since done practically the same thing. The bankers of some eight or ten little Tennessee towns put out 124,000 eggs on a plan similar to this in the spring of 1925.

That it is to the advantage of a town for the farmers of its trade territory to get the best possible prices for their products would seem to be a fact too obvious for anyone to argue about. That the typical country town has given much thought to or put much effort into the securing of this best possible price for the products of its tributary farms, is something few would dare to claim.

TOWN MARKETS AND FARMER MARKETMEN

One other phase of marketing remains a continuing source of town and country disagreement.

When the farmer comes to town to sell his produce direct to town consumers, probably in competition with the town merchants, what arrangements shall be made about it and how shall the farmer be treated?

Abundant efforts have been made to answer this question. Some towns have answered it, seemingly, to a fair degree of mutual satisfaction. Others have given answers not at all satisfactory to the marketing farmers. Some few have answered it in a manner more satisfactory to the marketing producers than to the town merchants. Changing conditions in many towns, too, have made the answers of one year unsatisfactory in later years.

It should not be an involved question, apparently, and yet it has its aspects of complexity. In the very small village the man from the country who has anything to sell generally just goes into town and sells it to whomever he can, and that is all there is to it. As the town gets larger, the merchant who sells potatoes and pork and butter and watermelons to the town householders is likely to find himself paying a rather stiff tax for the privilege of so doing. Then he begins questioning the justice of allowing the man from the country to come to town and sell the same products from house to house, at a slightly lower figure, perhaps, than he cares to meet. His feeling against the practice is likely to be intensified when, as often happens, the professional huckster begins to do business the farmer's way, maybe passing himself off for the grower of the stuff he sells to the folks who do not know him. If the grocerymen of the town have sufficient influence, there comes about this stage of town development, a "city ordinance" putting a license tax on farmers who do house to house peddling. In some states, I believe, ordinances of this kind attempting to reach farmers selling their own produce have been held void; possibly they would be so held anywhere, but the effort has been made, and may be made again. Naturally enough, when it is made, the farmers who have been doing this sort of business resent it. The right to sell whatever they have to sell, wherever they can sell it, and without paying for the privilege is likely to be thought of as an inherent right. Even where ordinances of this kind not primarily aimed at the farmer happen to touch him, they are resented. Much country feeling against the town has resulted from just this thing.

In the larger towns, the public market place is commonly looked to as the meeting point for country producers and town consumers. The open curb market into which the farmer drives his wagon for a certain number of hours, selling his produce direct to the housewife without payment of fees of any kind, is justly looked upon as the most practical answer to the question of what to do with the farmer when he comes to town to sell his stuff. The merchant who sells the same produce seldom objects to these markets; he is likely to favor them, indeed, and in most cases where there is a thriving retail curb market for the farmers there will be found alongside it an equally thriving stall market in which the town's merchants sell produce at practically the same prices as the farmers outside. This central trading place is as good for these merchants as it is for the farmers; and in one or two cases I have known, it was the merchants rather than the farmers who busied themselves about driving out of the "market square" the wholesale-buying and retail-selling traders who put their wagons on with those of the producers and posed as growers.

That the public market has been, and is, a good thing for all parties concerned is beyond question. The town with a live public market is always proud of it, and with reason. It gives the farmer the chance he must have to sell his stuff, and it gives the consumer the chance he should have to buy that stuff at a reasonable price. Even when there is friction between the town and the growers as to rules, and so on, the value of the market will be recognized by all.

Yet there is reason to think it would be well for both consumer and producer to consider this market proposition a bit more carefully in most towns, and to see whether or not it is the economical method of transferring farm products to town consumers that it is generally supposed to be.

It is well known that to any market of size come the growers who prefer to sell wholesale—that is, to dispose of their loads in large quantities to the grocers—as well as the growers who expect to sell in small quantities direct to the household buyers. It is not unusual, either, to find the more prosperous growers preferring the wholesale method. Mention has been made of the fact that in most markets where both farmer-sellers and merchants congregate prices are likely to be about or quite the same at the farmer's wagon as at the merchant's counter. This of itself is sometimes a cause of feeling on the part of the town consumer; he, or more often she, feels that the farmer could sell cheaper than the merchant if he would, and that in holding his prices up to the level of the merchants he is seeking to obtain undue profits.

This opinion is seldom justified by the facts. There are two main reasons for the farmer's failure to undersell his merchant competitor in the public market. One is that the market may exist largely by the good-

will of the merchants, and that any general attempt
by the farmers to undersell would result in setting the
merchant against the whole market proposition. The
other, and more important, is that retail selling, as
it is usually done on a public market, is an expensive business. The farmer who has to stay on the
market most of the day, and a good part of the night,
keeping his horses and his wagon, or his truck, there
with him, is at no inconsiderable expense as compared
with the volume of business he does. He must be paid
for his time if he is to make any profit from his
marketing; and it is seldom indeed that he becomes
rich from it. The grower who comes to town simply
to sell his load to the merchants and who sells and
gets back home as quickly as he can, is likely to have
the better of it. Both truck growers and truck consumers have a chance to profit, it would seem, by the
organization of the growers into some system of local
co-operative marketing that would leave the selling of
the produce of many growers to be done by a few
persons acting as their agents. Beyond question, distribution costs on most public markets could be sharply cut by such co-operation.

But that is another, even though a related, story.
The point right here is that, even though it is essential for the farmer to take his produce to town to
sell it, and even though the majority of townsmen
may desire that he bring and sell it directly to them,
there is often disagreement as to the conditions under
which it shall be offered for sale, and the regulations
by which the seller shall be governed. The town that

feels itself to have reached the dignity of licensing
and regulatory enactments, and that has not provided
the nearby farmer with an established marketing
place, owes it to itself as much as to the farmer to
consult with the growers, especially if those growers
be organized, in the working out of policies and rules
that shall be fair to all concerned. Many of the little
disagreements about policies and regulations of town
markets would be avoided, too, if the control of the
market were a joint matter between town and country, or even if the right of the growers to be heard
in an advisory capacity were recognized.

Certainly, if the farmer desires to bring his produce to town, the townsman equally desires to have
him bring it. To make him feel that the town wel-
comes him and that any rules or regulations it may
have made are for his protection as well as for its
own, is a better policy for the town than to vex
him with restrictions he does not understand or un-
necessarily to hamper in any way the free flow of
his products consumerward.

Closely related to this matter of marketing regulations is the matter of city health protection—the
inspection or oversight the town feels obliged to
insist on for the country products coming to town
to be offered for sale. Most towns have justification for the regulations they have made to govern
the production and sale of milk, for example, or
the slaughter and marketing of meat animals. Many
towns need more regulations of this sort, and a more
careful enforcement of the ones they have. Now and

then some town may enact an unreasonable ordinance; but oftener it is the country objection to the measure for health protection that is unreasonable. Yet even here, it would be no more than fair for the country, as an interested party, to be consulted about any proposed statute or ruling. Certainly, it would promote good feeling and a willingness to comply with requirements if the effort were made to explain to the countrymen affected the reason for any measure of this kind; and in some cases objectionable and unnecessary features and methods of enforcement might be obviated by getting the country point of view before framing the statute.

FARMER CO-OPERATION AND TOWN INTERESTS

One of the great economic developments of recent years is the growth of farmer co-operation. According to figures of the U. S. Department of Agriculture there were in the United States in November, 1926, 10,803 farmers' co-operative societies or associations with a total membership of about 2,700,000. These co-operative associations did in 1925, a business of some $2,400,000,000. These organizations are of various kinds. There are co-operative stores, there are mutual fire insurance companies, there are co-operative purchasing associations, and co-operative livestock improvement organizations. The great majority of the co-operatives, however, are primarily marketing organizations. They exist to help the farmer sell some one or other of his products to better advantage. These marketing associations are of very diverse types. Some of them—the co-operative creamery, for example, and the livestock shipping association, and the grain elevator—are primarily local organizations. Others, such as the great tobacco marketing associations, or the cotton associations, extend into a number of states and seek to have the deciding voice in the marketing of some great staple commodity. Some local industries—the raisin growing industry of California, or the walnut growing industry of the same state—are already so thoroughly organized that the co-operative is in virtual control of the commodity marketing. Some of the associations are based on a binding contract covering a term of years. Others are kept together only by a "gentleman's agreement," or by the profit that comes from doing business through them. Some of them are demonstrated successes. Others are still in the experimental stage. Some have failed, but the number of co-operative failures over a term of years is smaller in proportion to the total number of them than the number of failures among individual and corporate enterprises.

I am not going into any discussion of the desirability of co-operative marketing, or of the various types of co-operative organization, or of the dealings between farmer and co-operative—I have done enough of that elsewhere. What I am trying to do here is to point out that this idea of co-operative marketing has established itself rather firmly in the farmer mind, and that some millions of farmers are busily engaged in demonstrating to themselves and to the world that the idea is a workable one. Personally, I think that they have already demonstrated it. Some co-operatives have failed—doubtless others will fail; some of the marketing plans now being tried out may prove to be poor plans—that was to be expected; some of the results anticipated from co-operative marketing may not be realized—there are those who yet expect impossibilities; but it is unthinkable that all the efforts at co-operative marketing should be given up, or that the agriculture of the country should go back to a purely individualistic and unregulated marketing of their products by unorganized farmers. The movement is almost certain to be in the other direction. Great as is the value of the farm products now sold co-operatively, this method of doing business is, I think it safe to say, just getting itself established. There is going to be much more of it.

Now, this great development has been brought about—speaking generally and at large—by the farmers themselves, without the aid of, often over the opposition of, the towns with which those farmers do business. This general statement is, of course, subject to many individual modifications. In some cases—many cases in the aggregate—a few townsmen, or even a majority of townsmen, have given active aid to the farmers who were seeking to put their marketing on a co-operative basis. Bankers, especially, have been helpful in many cases in the establishment of both big and little co-operatives; and business men of all classes have here and there helped to carry on these co-operatives after they were established. Still, as a general proposition, the town has been against farmer co-operation. It still is, especially against any new form of co-operative marketing activity.

The town that has seen a co-operative creamery doing business for years is likely to believe in that form of co-operation; but the same town may give scant encouragement to a livestock shipping association or a tobacco marketing association. In too many cases farmers have come to accept the opposition of the town to any attempt at an improvement of farm marketing methods as a matter of course.

There are two great reasons for the town's taking this point of view and this stand.

The first is the instinctive distrust of new and untried methods of doing the thing one has become accustomed to seeing done according to accepted rules and methods—sheer conservatism, in a word; and conservatism is at once the preserver of the world and the greatest hindrance to its progress. The town is not to be condemned for remaining sanely conservative when new theories of marketing are offered and new policies proposed. The other reason for town opposition to co-operative marketing by farmers is that every successful co-operative, almost without exception, reduces the immediate profits of some man in town. The grain elevators have lessened the profits of the local grain dealers; co-operative shipments of livestock and poultry leave the local stock and poultry buyers without their accus-

tomed business; the success of the Burley Tobacco
Association in its early years put numbers of ware-
housemen and agent buyers and "pinhookers" out of
business. The men whose livelihood is thus inter-
fered with can scarcely be expected to support the
new movement; and too often these men, though
there may be only two or three of them in a town,
are able to carry with them the general sentiment of
the town and to set it against the efforts of the farmers to establish co-operative marketing. They are
able to do this because of the mistaken feeling of
town loyalty that bounds the town by its corporate
limits and fails to see in the farmer outside those
limits the reason for the trader within the town.

Many crimes have been committed in the name of
co-operation; many unsound schemes have been presented to the farmers by the overly enthusiastic or by
the unscrupulous; many exaggerated ideas as to the
money townsmen make out of the farmer's products
and as to the money the farmers can get through
co-operative marketing have been advanced. The
business men of the town are not called on to throw
themselves into any and every co-operative cam-
paign without due investigation of what it proposes
to do and of who is back of it. In some campaigns
they may need to remain in the opposition. In others,
however, they are needed in the ranks of the co-
operatives—needed both to help establish an institution that will be of benefit to the farmers and to help
guide and restrain it in its early days. Some towns-

men have rendered valiant service along both those lines; others could.

It is not to be expected that all the business men of a town will be able to see a proposed co-operative organization of farmers just in the same light. It is not necessary that they should. All the farmers will not agree about it. The important thing is that the townsman should recognize the importance of this movement, and should study it honestly, dispassionately, and with a thought to the welfare of the farmers about the town as well as to that of the merchants and traders in the town. As a class, townsmen have not yet done this; and the feeling that they have not, but have opposed it from selfish reasons only, has sprung up in the minds of many farmers and made them resentful. This state of things is unfortunate for all concerned; for here is one of the places in which mutual understanding and mutual confidence will make for the best interests of all.

The towns, the business men of the towns especially, owe it to themselves to know more about farmer co-operation and to put into their dealings with co-operating farmers more breadth of view and more thought for others than most of them have yet shown.

Chapter VI

SOME POLITICAL DIFFERENCES

A CITY COMPLAINT AGAINST THE COUNTRY

Lately I read a magazine article in which the case
of the city against the country was set forth in much
detail and with considerable acerbity. At least three
other magazines within a few months published articles along the same line. These articles were not of
great importance except as evidence of a growing
feeling on the part of many townsmen against what
they consider the too great power of the countryman
in politics. Cities and city dwellers often feel, and
sometimes justly feel, that they are "put upon" by
the country districts in a political way, that the country voter has entirely too much to do with things that
are solely the city's concern. They resent this, and
with it the fact that in numerous cases the vote cast
by the farmer counts for much more in determining
state policy than does the vote cast by the man in the
city.

Let us consider a few of the complaints made in
this particular article:

New York City, with a big majority of the state's
population, is still in a minority in both branches of
the state legislature. Chicago is in exactly the same
unhappy condition. Connecticut has a country town
of 257 souls equal with a city of 162,000 in the elec-
tion of members to the lower branch of the legisla-

ture. New Jersey's populous cities are under the control of "the yokels of the pine barrens." Delaware and Maryland cities are delivered by old legislative apportionments into the hands of the back counties. Worst of all, in Rhode Island 17,807 people in the thirteen rural towns outvote more than half a million people in eleven cities.

Nor has this "hayseed minority," we learn as the tale proceeds, been inclined to use its power with either courtesy or discretion. It has not hesitated to deny the cities the privileges they desired or to force upon them laws they did not desire. In state after state, it has defeated Daylight Saving Acts much desired by city folks. It has turned the control of Boston's police force over to the state. It has insisted on limiting municipal indebtedness and municipal expenditures, often to the serious inconvenience of the municipalities affected. It has forced prohibition on unwilling majorities. It passes laws that take tax money from the cities for the rural districts.

These are true charges on the whole. Let me, as one of the rural folks, confess, too, that I have seen the countrymen of my own state legislate for the state's cities with little regard for city wishes or feelings. The state's first prohibition law was passed over the bitter protest of the larger cities—which for quite a while openly disregarded it. The Sunday movie has been barred in towns that desired it. The attempt is repeatedly made to stop Sunday baseball in cities that wish to keep it. And all of our urban counties, when they think of the automobile taxes their citi-

zens pay to build roads in the backwoods counties,
lift up their voices and make a mournful wail.

THE COUNTRY'S REJOINDER

Of course this inequality of voting power ought
not to be. There can be no justification of the sys-
tems of apportionment which in some states give a
country minority a more potent voice in the conduct
of state affairs than the city majority has. Nor can
there be any convincing argument made for the right
of distant country districts to decide for a city
whether or not it shall have Sunday movies and
Sunday baseball, or how its policemen shall be
chosen and what they shall be paid.

Yet in practically every case in which they possess
either the power of outvoting the cities, while having
fewer votes, or of interfering in concerns that are
purely city concerns, the farmer voters remain quite
unwilling to give up this power. They cling to it
even when they do not attempt to justify it.

In some cases this desire to hold more than is their
own comes largely from partisan feeling. The country districts go for one party, the towns for another.
This is largely responsible for the continuance of
Rhode Island's absurd "rotten borough" system of
choosing members of the state legislature. But parti-
sanship is not the only reason for the countryman's
insistence on holding the whip hand whenever he
can. Nor is the mere reluctance all humanity feels
toward the giving up of any power it possesses—
even unjust power—the only reason. There is another
feeling to be considered along with these two.

The countryman, I am persuaded, clings to whatever power he may have over the city, however unfair the exercise of that power may seem, partly, at least, from a certain vague instinct or impulse of self-preservation. He rules the city when he can because he is very much afraid to have the city rule him.

This fear is not without justification. For if it be true—as it is—that the farmer does not understand all the city man's problems and is prone to apply backwoods standards to metropolitan circumstances and conditions, it is equally true that the city does not understand many of the country's problems and can not be trusted to deal with them with any more fairness or any more intelligence than the country displays in dealing with the things that are exclusively the city's. It is unquestionably bad—in both theory and practice—for rural New York or "down state" Illinois to have the power to interfere with matters that directly concern only Manhattan or Chicago. It is contrary to one of the cardinal tenets of Americanism for the rural minority of those states to outvote the urban majority in their legislatures. Yet conditions might be worse if the situation were reversed and the cities were free to do what they liked with affairs particularly the farmer's.

The country, too, needs protection from outside dictation. There are special country interests to consider as well as special city interests. There are times, too, when it is no denial of either justice or democracy to limit the powers of the majority.

Take the matter of Daylight Saving, for example. To the city man it no doubt seems a simple matter for everybody to turn his clock up an hour when the long days come, for business generally to be done earlier in the day, and for all to enjoy the hour of evening leisure that may thus be made available. It is not a simple matter to the farmer; it is a very vexatious matter, and often a very expensive one. He does not need to start his day earlier, and he is decidedly a loser when he shifts whatever leisure period he may have from the early morning to the late afternoon. An hour just before sunset is worth much more to him than an hour just after sunrise. Countrymen have weather to consider, and dews, and things of that kind. The haymaker or the harvester goes to the field as the sun and clouds dictate and not by the orders of the clock. To do at six o'clock the thing he has been used to do at seven, means something more to the man in the country than an agreeable change of routine. It probably means an upsetting of his whole schedule and the exchange of a convenient and valuable hour for one that is neither so convenient nor so valuable.

"If groups of folks in the city wish to get at their work an hour earlier in the summer, and so gain an hour for recreation in the evening," the farmer has argued, "let them simply move up their office or factory hours and not try to move up all the processes of life, including the processes of us who are now starting the day earlier than anybody else, and who can only be discommoded and injured by the change."

And the farmer has been right about it. The good
Daylight Saving has done others has not compensated for the harm it has done him. So he has used
his surplus of political power wherever he had it to
stop the whole business. An unfair exercise of power
in some cases beyond all doubt; and yet it is fortunate, on the whole, that he has been able to use it.

Or take prohibition. Generally speaking, the country has favored prohibition, the cities opposed it.
Rural communities wishing to get rid of the saloon
tried local option first. It was the perfect solution—
in theory. "Let the communities that wish the saloon
keep them, the communities that do not wish them do
away with them." It looked easy.

But it did not work out so well. The saloon in the
town catered to country appetites as well as to city
appetites. The effects of the thing did not stop when
the dry line was reached. "Wherefore," said the
countryman, "the saloon is a bad thing anyway, and
it keeps on hurting us, so we will just do away with
it altogether." And he did. The reasoning may not
be without flaw, but whether or not he believes prohibition a good thing, one must admit that there is in
the argument a sort of rough logic that is not without force. The countryman has been looking after
his own and not altogether meddling with someone
else.

Let not any reader imagine that I would argue that
the countryman has always been right, or that he
possesses any superior civic virtue. He has probably

been wrong just about as often as he has been right, and as I have said, it is against our sense of fair play for the votes of one class to be made to count for more than an equal number of votes cast by another class. A remedy for that state of things should be found. It is not easy either to compound or to administer this remedy; but the thing is not impossible. A greater degree of home rule for cities, with a corresponding constitutional protection for rural districts, immediately suggests itself as a desirable prescription; but it is not always easy to apply even this palliative. Mutual education of town and country to the special needs of each must be depended on finally to remove the trouble. Town and country need each other's co-operation—and probably each other's opposition at times—in the settling of questions that concern them both; while there are other questions which each must agree to leave the other to settle for itself.

The formation of separate states out of great cities such as New York and Chicago has been suggested. There are many arguments in favor of such division, and one really potent argument against it. The rural districts should not, can not in any justice, be deprived of the tax revenue which the great cities are able to pay and the country is not.

The cities have cause of complaint when the farmers try to run municipal affairs; but when those cities complain because tax money goes from the city to help build roads and equip schools and preserve order in the country, they need an elementary course in economics and sociology—and common sense.

THE COUNTRY TOWN AS MEDIATOR

All this, it might be objected, is a discussion of country and city differences, and not a discussion of the country town at all. There would be truth in such objection, too; but the country town is interested, just the same, in the disputes between city and country and in the way they may be settled.

In these political conflicts, as well as in the conflicts of business, the town has first of all to determine whether it will consider itself as belonging with the city or with the country, whether it is more interested in seeing the great city grow or in seeing the neighboring countryside prosper. The rule has been, I think, for the little town to think in city terms; for the country town banker or merchant or professional man to feel that in any conflict of interests between city and country he should help fill up the ranks led by his fellow business men in the city, rather than range himself alongside the farmers living about him. Most that has been so far said in this book has been said in an effort to demonstrate that this feeling is a mistaken one; that, as between city and country, the small town business man is really part of the country and should so feel and so conduct himself. It is from the country and not from the city that he gets his living; it is to the country and not to the city that he must look for the materials of growth that will make his town larger and more prosperous.

This is not saying that the man in the country town should as a matter of course support every political demand of the country or pander to its every feeling. The country is wrong, both politically and economically, a good part of the time; country feeling is not always a safe political guide. Indeed, the city has more than once saved the country from itself; and the country needs as leaders—always, and in politics as well as in business—men who have had city contacts and who can look at matters from the city point of view as well as from that of the country. The man in the country town should be able much oftener than he is to give wise counsel and to be a sane leader; but before he can do or be this with much effect he must know the country viewpoint and the country needs, and must realize his real relationship with the country. So long as he thinks of himself as a sort of exile from the city, and of his town as a sort of commercial oasis in a desert of agriculture, he is not going to accomplish much as a leader of farmers. And it is well that he should not.

The country town, too, has often some of the very same political disagreements with the country about it that the cities as a group have with the agricultural sections as a whole. The town is often conservative politically when the country is progressive, and just as often it is progressive in regard to other matters on which the country is conservative. Little towns find themselves disputing with the farmers around them about roads, and schools, and police regulations, and market privileges, and a score of other matters. The town that owns its own lighting or water plant has, as a rule, a perennial source of disagreement with the folks beyond "city limits" who want light

or water. The townsman in a rural county is likely
to feel himself without the proper voice in the county
court or on the county commission. The farmer, coming to the place where the county road stops and the
town paving does not yet begin, is likely to feel a
bit of resentment toward the town folks who make
him drive over bumps and through ruts and chug-
holes. The. man within the city limits, thinking of
highway taxes he must pay but which may not be
expended within the town, has a feeling, probably
suppressed, that he is being taxed for another's
benefit.

WHO PAYS THE TAXES?

This matter of taxes, who shall pay them, and who
shall have the benefit of them, is the great source of
political disagreement between classes, and occupa-
tions, and localities.

Every now and then some statesman from New
York, or Pennsylvania, or Massachusetts, rises up
with a lot of figures to show how much more income
tax his state pays than is paid by a whole bunch of
Southern or Western states; and often he does a
regular "sob stunt" about it. There seems to be, the
nation over, a sort of feeling in cities, even in little
country towns, that the town is taxed for the benefit of the farmer. There is the same feeling on the
part of the wealthy that they are taxed for the benefit of the poor. The poor, of course, are equally certain that the thing works the other way. So are the
farmers. "The farmer pays too large a share of the

taxes," is a common complaint in every rural district. Against the grumbling of the Northeast about the income and inheritance taxes it has to pay into the National Treasury, may be placed the growls of the agricultural South and West about the many millions taken from them in tariff tolls to help enrich the manufacturing centers,

Now, when one goes to discussing taxes and taxation, he is far more likely to stir up opposition than to secure assent; and when he starts to replying to objections and to contradictions, he lets himself in for endless argument. I am not going to argue tax questions, I am not even going to discuss them at any length. I wish to call attention to just one or two fundamental facts and to express my opinion on one or two matters of policy which seem to me of prime importance.

Despite all the burdens that have been laid on wealth in the way of heavy income and inheritance taxes, the poor are still more heavily taxed than the rich. Despite the seemingly higher rates and the special taxes so often imposed on the urban districts, the farming sections still pay more than their fair share of taxes into state and Federal treasuries.

One might pile up a mass of statistics to support these broad assertions; but other statistics could be piled up to disprove them. Figures can be made to do almost anything for an ingenious man. Passing by the whole fertile field of statistics and of argument, I prefer to let the first of these propositions rest on the fact that the centralization of wealth continues;

the second, on the fact that the towns continue to grow in wealth much more rapidly than the country.

As to what taxation could or should do to check either of these tendencies, is not a question to be argued here. The point is that it is not yet, so far as we can see, checking either of them. The two tendencies are necessarily interrelated and correlative, since the very wealthy, as well as the mass of wealth, gravitate to the city.

The rich do not pay as much tax as they think, and neither do the urban districts. It is idle for anyone to complain about, or to claim credit for, paying a tax that he can and does shift to others. Income taxes and corporation taxes are not always shifted from the man or the corporation directly paying them to that man's or that corporation's customers or employees; but they are often so shifted. The tariff tax the laborer pays when he buys a suit of clothes or a bag of sugar, is paid by him, absolutely and with finality. The landlord does not pay the taxes on his buildings, the tenants pay them. If the landlord owns a vacant lot, he expects the general public to pay the taxes on it—as it usually does with something over; else he would not hold it. The merchant passes his privilege and *ad valorem* taxes on to his customers; these taxes are part of his running expenses. The public usually pays the taxes of public service corporations. But the farmer seldom has any means by which he can make somebody else pay the tax on his real estate or his personal property. He is a real taxpayer. Sometimes farming lands are as-

sessed for a much smaller proportion of their selling
value than is some of the real estate in town; and
this is often urged against the farmer by townfolk.
Because of the difference in their ability to shift
taxes, however, this apparent discrimination in favor
of the farmer profits him much less on the whole
than the townsman supposes, though it must be admitted that the city home-owner largely shares the
farmer's inability to pass his real estate tax on to
some one else. When it comes to direct taxes on personal property, it is notorious that the farmer pays
much more than his share. It is doubtful if there is
a state, or even a county, levying such a tax in
which this is not the rule. The National Industrial
Conference Board estimated that in 1922 the farmers
paid out 16.6 per cent of their share of the national
income in taxes; the rest of the business community,
11.9 per cent of its share.

Tax inequalities and injustices are things we have
not yet learned to correct or avoid. It is doubtful if
we shall be able to get rid of them before the Millen-
ium. Patriotism and wise forethought both demand,
however, that we do our best to reduce them to the
minimum. This we shall not do until all of us—the
majority of us, at least—learn to think of them less
as matters of individual concern and more as matters
of principle, and until we make an honest endeavor
to consider the circumstances and the viewpoint of
the other men and the other classes and the other
sections that must also pay taxes.

The townsman can well afford to give some

thought to this matter of country versus town taxation. It is seldom that the man in town, or the dollar in town, pays more taxes proportionately than the man or the dollar in the country, and the recognition of this fact by the country town could not but be good for it.

THE SPENDING OF THE TAX MONEY

Louder and more general than the complaint made by cities and towns over the taxes they have to pay is the complaint they make over the spending in the country of this tax money. It is not only that his section pays the bulk of the income and inheritance taxes that the statesman from the industrial East complains about, but more particularly and vociferously that so much of these taxes is spent on all sorts of policies and projects designed for the benefit of Western and Southern farmers and villagers. In every state the larger cities still tell the same doleful story about the spending of the taxes they pay out in the rural districts. "Pauper counties," meaning the counties that get more from the state treasury than they pay into it, are sneered at in state legislatures and in small city newspapers. In any country town, almost, can be found someone who can demonstrate that the town is being taxed to help keep up the "back districts." Small town business men who object to the spending of county funds to keep a farm agent "for the benefit of the farmers" are not yet an extinct race.

These complaints, considering only the number of

dollars actually paid in taxes by cities and by the country, are based on facts. The cities, the small towns even, do not get back all of the tax money they pay, or seem to pay. Some of it is spent in the country.

It is one thing, however, to admit this fact, and another thing to find fault with it. Remembering the concentration of wealth in the towns and cities, remembering the larger proportion of children in the country, remembering the greater distances of the country and the consequently greater expense per capita of providing there the same governmental protection and the same facilities for transportation and education, it becomes at once evident that the country must look to the town to pay a part of the running expenses of the government machinery in the open spaces. More tax money than the country with its smaller number of people and smaller per capita wealth can reasonably be expected to pay must be spent in the country if the difference between opportunity and privilege in town and country, already too great, is not steadily to increase. The poorer country districts simply have not the money with which to provide for themselves the things modern civilization demands—good schools, good roads, efficient public health service, adequate police protection, and so on. The money to provide these things must come, in part at least, from the towns. It is but fair and just that it should. Not only because the town really pays less and the country more than its apparent share of taxes, but also because the town has been devel-

oped by and will continue to be supported by the country. The tax money the town sends into the country
will, in large measure, come back to it. Even should
it not, the town has a vital concern in all that is
taking place among its tributary fields and wood-
lands, and is no more suffering injustice when it
sends money out of its own pocket to help assure
civilization in the backwoods than is the heart when
it pumps the life blood of the body out into hands
and feet.

Chapter VII

SCHOOLS, CHURCHES, AND ROADS

TOWN SCHOOLS AND COUNTRY ROADS

Town schools, the nation over, are better than country schools. If there is an exception to this general rule here and there, it is but an exception. The rule holds good, and it is of so general application that we have come to think of it as a matter of course. We take it for granted that the town will have larger and more attractive schoolhouses than the country districts, that these better buildings will be better equipped, that the schools will run more weeks in the year, that better teachers will be employed to teach in them, and that these teachers will draw larger salaries than country teachers receive. In most states it is taken for granted even that the country children of counties in which there are large towns will have better schools, longer terms, more efficient teachers, than the country children of counties in which there are no sizable towns. Even now, though less often than formerly, the school provisions made for the children of a particular county may vary greatly between the more prosperous districts and the poorer ones.

The average city child of the United States has a school term eight full weeks longer (182 days against 142 days) than that of the average country child. Elementary school teachers in cities of 100,000 and more population draw an average annual salary of $1,968. This average runs downward with the size of the city; but even in the village of 2,500 to 5,000 it is $1,129. In the two-teacher country schools it is $742; in the one-teacher country schools, but $735.

Length of school terms, salaries of teachers, standards of equipment have all increased notably the nation over these latter years; but less progress has been made in all these respects in the isolated districts than anywhere else. Some rural communities, through consolidation, special local taxation, or other means, have made great progress toward better educational opportunities the past decade or two; but it is not hard at all to find other communities in which progress has been negligible.

There is reason for this state of things. Good business and good equipment are called for and provided for when a thousand children go to the same school. Cut the number down to a hundred, and if the school money is raised by a property tax, as it usually is, it will not be so easy to provide equally good equipment. Go "way back" into the country district, where the families are scattered, the children few, and either the land poor or the marketing conditions bad —one or the other of these will be found in practically every "way back" neighborhood—and there can be only a small investment in the educational plant. Unless there is some outside contribution to help out that of the neighborhood itself, there will be but a shabby building, a short term of school, and a cheap teacher in charge of the school.

It is manifestly impossible for the poor-soiled or the thinly settled rural county of itself to provide good schools for its children. It simply has not the money with which to do it. The differences between the per capita wealth of one county and that of another are likely to startle one who never has thought of it. One does not have to go to the great cities to find these differences, either. For every school child in Forsyth County, N. C., there was in 1925, $8,444 of taxable wealth; for every child in Guilford County, $6,090; for every child in Franklin County, $1,565; for every child in Wilkes County, $1,513. Usually, too, the poor county has no great will to tax itself unduly to school its children. The people who most truly value education and educational opportunities are likely to be elsewhere than in the poorer country districts. Back into these districts, instead, have been crowded the people who, because of their own lack of ability or of opportunity, have failed to keep up with the world. Many a poor county or community, with the passage of years, becomes relatively poorer than its physical conditions would justify chiefly because it has become an educational and intellectual backwash.

Now, if it be true—and it is—that the unnecessary poverty of any country district means an unnecessary lessening of business in some town, it is evident that every town has a direct and decided interest in the education of all the children of its trade territory. The poor schools of the back districts concern it.

Aside from this interest, too, there must be consideration of the rights of the children concerned. There are yet those people who believe that a child's school opportunities should be determined by the wealth or poverty of the immediate locality in which the child chances to live; but the feeling of the time is coming more and more to be that the child is born of the state as well as of the neighborhood, and that the state should not play the neglectful step-mother toward any of its children. If Jimmy Brown and Susie Jones, living just over the line in Bigtown County, have a right to go to school eight months in the year, it is hard to see why Tommy Smith and Mary Clark, just across the road in Littleburg County, should have a chance to go only five months in a year. Indeed, many are beginning to question whether there is not something unfair in a system that provides a nine months' school for the child just inside the city limits and only a seven months' school for the child just outside those limits. "In rural communities," says the U. S. Bureau of Education, "the school term is shorter, the instruction of a poorer quality, fewer children finish high school and college. This situation is contrary to the spirit of our Constitution. It is not only unjust, but unnecessary." Many not in official station are coming to think the same way. Probably the stage of absolute educational equality between town and country will never be reached; possibly an absolute equality is not even to be desired; but that there must be less of inequality is coming to be generally accepted.

Existing inequalities can be lessened only by making the towns, the centers of wealth and population, contribute more than they have been contributing to the schools of the country districts in which people are few and property values low. Some counties, some large rural sections even, can hope to secure the schools the times have come to demand only through liberal state aid. Such counties or sections will be found in a majority of all the states.

The townsman, then, is called upon, both as a business man and as a patriot, to contribute even more liberally than he has been contributing to the equalization of the educational opportunities offered country children with the opportunities enjoyed by his own children. He is asked to consent that more of his tax money go to educate the children of others— children, perhaps, of people he does not even know. Can he afford to do this thing? Is it just that he be asked to do it?

Yes, to both questions, and for reasons given in the preceding chapter. The line between town and country is an artificial line; the line between county and county often an imaginary one. Just as the state is less motherly than a state should be if any child is denied opportunity because of local poverty, so the man in town is less of a citizen than he should be if he limits his civic interests by his corporation's boundary lines.

THE IGNORANCE THAT DESTROYS

The townsman should make this contribution to country schools not only without ungracious protest, but with real willingness. He can afford to do it. He is paying to educate the town's future citizens as well as future countrymen when he does it. Some of those back-country children are certainly coming to town, and the more they know and the more they can do when they come, the more they will be worth to the town.

He can afford to do it also on the broader ground that he will be helping to reduce ignorance; and ignorance is contagious and reactive.

The town has much it could and should teach to the country. It has acquired knowledge that the country has not acquired, and that it would be good for the country to have. If the farmer knew more of the processes involved in the daily work of the merchant or the banker or the city laborer, there would be less feeling against these men in the country. Understanding between town and country would be easier to arrive at; misunderstandings and bad feelings would be more easily cleared away. The more the country learns about the town and its people, the better it will understand the town point of view and the more clearly it will comprehend the townsman's problems. It is easier to carry a message to a people who have been taught and who have learned to think than to a people who are yet ignorant, or who trust in prejudice rather than in reason.

The town, too, needs to learn from the country. The countryman knows a lot of things that the townsman has never known or has forgotten. The farmer has his particular problems, and needs knowledge not only to help him solve those problems but also to help him present them to others. Instruction should come to the town from the country as well as go out to the country from the town. The more the country knows the more it can tell the town, and the more accurate what it tells is likely to be.

For always it is to be kept in mind that ignorance, wherever it may be, is dangerous and destructive. "For lack of knowledge is my people destroyed." The lack of knowledge that burns off the forests, or sets the hillsides to gullying, or promotes an epidemic of typhoid is a matter of concern not only to the community directly affected, but to the larger community, to the state, to the nation.

All knowledge does not come out of the schools or go into them. Town schools and country schools alike, they are yet far from perfect institutions. They probably teach some things they should not teach, and they certainly leave untaught some things that should be taught. Still, most people get their start toward knowledge—toward education even—in the schools. They are the most effective disseminators of useful knowledge we have; and they are improving as our ideals and conceptions advance. To strengthen them is to make possible a finer civilization for to-morrow. They are saving forces, unremitting enemies of the ignorance that destroys. Not the least important of them may be the little school at Wayback, where the thin fields run out into the woods. The tax money that goes to make that school efficient strikes at ignorance in its very lair.

The townsman can afford to carry the fight for education to the far frontiers.

THE TOWN AND THE COUNTRY CHURCH

In many instances the country child is being taken to town for his schooling. In many other instances new educational centers are being established in the country for his benefit. Sentiment still clings about the "little red schoolhouse," or even about the little unpainted and weather-beaten schoolhouse that sits—

> "By the road,
> A ragged beggar sunning"—

but this sentiment is not being allowed to blind all the people to the fact that there is a better chance to give efficient instruction when comparatively large groups of children are brought together. Sentiment clings, too, about—

> "The little brown church in the wildwood"—

and about—

> "The tiny white spire
> From the green glen up-pointing"—

but here again sentiment cannot always be made the deciding factor.

There is a limit to the extent to which the consolidation of country schools can, and should, be carried. There is still, and will long remain, a place for the little one-room schoolhouse with its dozen or so pupils clustered about the "single, sole, and solitary" teacher. So there will long remain a place for the little isolated country church. The taking of the country children to town to school, even when they find a better school there, is not an unmixed good. Neither will be the taking of farm folks to town to church; but this seems in a great number of cases the only way out of a bad situation.

That the country church is, generally speaking, in a bad way is generally agreed. As to what are the reasons for its being in this bad way, there is general disagreement. The opinion of each man is likely to rest upon conditions in his own neighborhood and upon his own religious convictions or his own theological prepossessions. To me, it seems that the church plays a much less important part in the lives of most people than it once did. Its religious ministrations may still belong to it alone; but the social needs it once met are now being largely met by other institutions. The farm family in most communities does not look forward to the weekly or semi-monthly trip to church as the social event of that week or those weeks, as it once did. Even where church-going is still a social as well as a religious function, social demands are larger, and are less fully supplied by the simple fact of seeing one's neighbors and talking over things with them. The church still remains an important social factor in the country; in many communities it is still probably the most important single factor. But in very few communities is it as important as it once was in this respect, and it is not likely again to be so. This is one of the reasons for the decline of the country church; and it is a reason for which civilization itself and not the church is to blame—if any blame attaches for what is a perfectly natural development.

Personally, I think, too, that the church has failed many country districts when it comes to the purely spiritual needs of those districts. The church is a conserving force rather than a progressing institution. In many cases it has been too conservative, and has failed to progress even as rapidly as the country about it and the people who must support it. The tendency for a church in a country neighborhood to pass into the control and remain under the direction of the neighborhood's more elderly citizens, and those of most fixed and unchanging practices of life, is perhaps an unavoidable tendency. It is a tendency that works for good in some ways. It also works for harm in other ways. Let the community grow beyond the preacher in knowledge and in understanding of life, and the preacher is not the important man in the community that he once was. Let a few persons in a neighborhood attempt to bind the church to an unyielding theology or an antiquated code of conduct, and the neighborhood will pay less and less attention to the warnings of the church and be less and less inclined to give it the financial support it must have. Even to mention these things is to trespass on disputed ground; but in an agricultural world that is thinking as never before of co-operation, a church that sets itself to dividing neighbor from neighbor, as too many country churches by their insistence on denominational differences surely do, is bound to lose influence. In a time that is looking

to and believing in the future as few times have looked and believed, a church that turns to the past for
all of its doctrine and all of its practices can not com-
mand enthusiastic support. And many country
churches are doing this very thing.

Another reason for the decline in power and influence of the church is the purely financial reason.
This accounts, too, for much of the church's waning
importance as a social center, and—rash as it may
seem to say it—for much of its decline as a spiritual
force.

It costs more than it once did to keep churches
going. The standards of public knowledge and of
required qualifications for public leaders of all kinds
have been raised, that for preachers along with
others. The type of preacher that once satisfied, or
was even desired, is not satisfactory now in most
cases; and men with the qualifications demanded of
the modern minister have not been preparing for the
ministry in adequate numbers. Such as have prepared themselves are taken up at once by the town
churches. In a word, there is not a sufficient number
of good, or even satisfying, preachers to supply all
the churches; and the city churches get the pick. The
country churches have to take what is left. Even
in the denominations which allot places to their ministers, the better preachers are sent to the larger and
wealthier city churches. It is inevitable that this
should be so. Country people may or may not be
less willing now than they once were to contribute
to their churches; but there can be no question that

they must contribute much more than they have ever given, and meet the stiffest sort of competition, if they are to stand even a chance of getting preachers comparable in natural ability and in training with the leaders in other lines of life.

Find a country church that is in a flourishing condition, and one of two other things is likely to be found. Either there will be a community in which the church, because of isolation, lack of social progress, or some other evident cause, fills its old place as the social center of the community, or there will be serving the church a preacher of outstanding ability to stir the hearts, gain the confidence, and influence the lives of his hearers.

The country church as a general proposition is failing to "carry on" both because it does not meet the demands of an advancing age and because it can not meet the financial competition of the church in town in securing its part of the insufficient supply of capable ministers.

Now, the town churches can not be expected to deprive themselves of the services of the most capable men in order that the country churches may prosper. Good preachers are none too common in the towns; and the towns, like the country, are over-churched. If the townsman is to do anything for the country church, he must in most cases do it by giving the countryman a share in the better things he has for himself. In a great many cases the practical proposition, it seems to me, is to bring the countryman to the town church. This can not be done always, of course; but it is being done to an increasing extent all the time. Automobiles and good roads have wiped out hours and distances and made it as practical often for the farmer to go fifteen or twenty miles to church in town as it used to be for him to go two or three miles to church in the country.

Rural America has more churches than it needs, or will attend, or can adequately support. Some years ago I passed through a little burg, a mere way station. Looking out the car window, I saw two little churches built almost exactly alike standing on opposite sides of the road. Turning a little, I saw a third one down the road a bit. I knew enough about that country to know that there could not be within attending distance of those three churches a sufficient number of people to pay preachers and meet the other expenses necessary to keep them going. I knew enough about it, too, to know that the two or three leading sects of the neighborhood were uncompromising in their doctrinal insistence and in their determination to go to Heaven each along its own particular road. Anyone could see that there were two superfluous churches there; but no one, I imagine, would have tried to get those devout country folks to unite to give the community one strong and well supported church. Certainly, no one would have added anything to his popularity in that neighborhood by suggesting such a thing.

Excessive sectarianism is, if the full truth could be learned, probably the greatest enemy practical and resultful religion has to face in our country districts.

It is not the people who have decided not to be good, but the people who are determined to be good only in their own way and among their exact counterparts in belief who are responsible for the great numbers of half-deserted churches in the farming sections. In many cases there must be the community church, as opposed to the church of this or that denomination, if there is to be in the community any church at all adequate to the work a church should do.

In this connection, many rural neighborhoods might profit by the example set by an Arkansas community I have visited. This community, made up of large farms and prosperous farmers, is near a city—so near that the farm owners belong to city clubs and go to town to lunch when they wish. But it has its own church. Just a neat little country church, but in it four ministers representing four different denominations preach regularly. There are adherents of each of the four sects in the community and all are treated alike. The whole community—landlords and tenants, alike—goes to church regularly; and the Sunday school is the neighborhood pride. There is a community church fund, and out of it the preachers are paid—each the same. Instead of fighting each other, the denominations work together; instead of dissipating its energy on more churches than it could decently support, the community has one church of which it is justly proud.

But this is a ticklish subject, as I have intimated. To some sects and to many country church mem-

bers, such co-operation would seem treason to the
faith. Inter-denominational unity or co-operation
concerns the question of town and country only as a
study of it may lead to the conclusion that the stress-
ing of religious differences instead of religious agree-
ments, however profitable it may be in town, is a
bad thing for the churches and for the progress of
Christianity in the country.

The townsman can best help the country church
by making it possible for the various sects to forget their differences, and by helping the countryman who may be within reach of the town church
to feel at home when he comes there. The church
should be a good place for people to meet and get
acquainted and come to an understanding—in the
country, it should be a good meeting place for the
man who is at home within the town and the stranger
from outside the gates, that is, from the country
farm.

This is one of the cases in which the town dweller
has more to offer the country dweller, as a rule,
than the country dweller has to offer the town
dweller. He is likely to have a more attractive and
comfortable house of worship, better preaching,
better music, the inspiration of a larger congrega-
tion. He should have to offer along with these an
amount of friendliness and welcome and real kindli-
ness of heart equal to that he would find in most
country churches—denominational differences not
interfering.

THE TOWN MUST HELP BUILD COUNTRY ROADS

The town can offer its church advantages to the country, at least to that part of the country within easy reach of it; but it can not take its streets and roads out to the country. The man from Wayback must travel Wayback's roads to reach town, and the man from town must journey over the same ways to reach Wayback.

Any road is a thing of interest to a great many people. To the man whose home it runs by, first of all; then to the man who travels it regularly; then to the occasional traveler of it; then in varying degree to all the people who in any way depend on or use the things that must be hauled over it. A good road is a prime economy; a bad road, a continual extravagance.

No section needs good roads more than the country district remote from the railways. None, left to itself, is as unlikely to have them.

Some few years since I went from the little Virginia village of R across country to the Tennessee village of S and from this some 30 miles across country to reach the railroad again. There are railroad points a bit nearer S than either of these! But the nearest railroad station is 22 miles away. Everything that is taken into the town must be hauled several miles over public roads. From R I went out ten miles in a Ford. It was a wonderful road, mostly a stone road—of Nature's building. The stones were large, and often declivitous. Once or twice we crossed hills and over these hills the roads were largely gullies, and the gullies were more than declivitous; they were precipitous. The young fellow who took me out was scared of the road, to be sure, and need not have taken all of the two and three-quarters hours he spent making the ten miles. He charged me $10 for making the trip. I protested, of course; but I was not so sure in my heart that he had not earned it, and I left him expressing doubts as to his ever getting back home. I trust he did. I know he could not have taken me the rest of the way; for no Ford could have negotiated the ridge I crossed. I rode over it horseback. The man who piloted me, knowing the road better than I, and probably having more sense, got off his horse at intervals to lead it around or through the mud-holes. I stayed on, and the Providence that looks after little children and grown-up fools brought me safely through. But I carried a good part of the ridge with me.

Another Ford took me out of S across the mountain on the other side. That was a fairly good mountain road; only twice we in our car had to get out and with the help of the men in the car just behind boost our car and theirs over slippery rocks and through mud banks.

This is an extreme case, to be sure, and a good road reaches nearer the village now; but there is many a mountain or back-country section to and from which the public road—and that a bad road—is the only means of ingress or egress. As with good schools, it is simply impossible for the people of these sections to provide roads for themselves. They have

no way to raise the money necessary to build roads.
Yet, lacking good roads, every productive activity
must be less profitable than it should be, every social
activity must be circumscribed and hampered. Where
is there greater need for roads, or where can the state
spend money to better advantage than in putting these
isolated districts into closer touch with the great
world outside?

The notion that each neighborhood should build
and keep up its own roads is an outgrown notion.
Increasing long-distance travel has made the highway something more than a local affair.

A few really local roads there may be yet—roads
which serve only the people who live along them;
but these roads are becoming fewer all the time,
and the main highways, on which most of the road
money is spent, become every year more of a general and less of a local possession. Changes in methods of collecting road taxes have not kept pace with
the change from horse-drawn, and therefore almost
entirely local, to motorized, and therefore largely
long-distance, traffic. It is true that county aid to the
neighborhood, state aid, Federal aid, have all come.
Local taxes and local forced labor are no longer expected to keep the main roads in repair. County and
state bond issues, automobile taxes, gasoline taxes,
are being utilized for road construction. They had to
come, since without them the roads demanded by an
automobiling nation would be impossible.

Personally, I believe that, since the building of a
good road by any piece of land increases the value

of that land, an abutting property tax should fur-
nish part—but only part—of the funds for all road
construction. No other tax could be juster; under no
other system, I am convinced, would as many good
roads be constructed. Cities everywhere build their
streets largely by such assessments. But since all
classes profit more or less by the building of good
roads, all classes should contribute to make them
possible.

The townsman's interest in roads does not end
with the end of his own streets, or even with the road
on which he and his family are in the habit of driving
of afternoons. That interest reaches out just as far
as the commodities of his town go, and just as far
as his town reaches out to draw to itself the farm
products it must have to keep it alive.

In my state a year or so ago there was quite a
fight over the apportionment of the automobile license
taxes. The larger counties, with the most automobiles
and the best roads, wished to keep the funds col-
lected from these license fees for their own use. The
less populous and poorer counties, with fewer automobiles and with worse roads, wished this tax money
to go into a state fund. The smaller counties won, as
they should have won; but the opposition seemed to
me to come from such a selfish and short-sighted
point of view that I could not but wish that the
legislators constituting this opposition had to live
a while in a town like S and get out of it, when they
had to go out, over such roads as I took into and
out of it. Or over a road like the one on which I

went another time from one Cumberland Plateau
town to another, a road that dipped itself down into
the gorge of a little river, winding itself so closely
along the edges of the chasm below that the elderly
lawyer who was in the seat with me sat on the upper
side of the car all the way down with the door open
and one foot outside it, ready to make a jump for
safety if the rest of us should take a tumble into
the depths below. Thinking of that opposition, I
wondered, too, how so many people have lived so
long in little towns surrounded by the open spaces
where live the scattered farm folks who make those
towns possible, without seeming ever to realize that
those farmers are a necessary part of the population
and that their needs and their desires are not greatly
different, after all, from those of the folks in town.

Chapter VIII

WHERE THE TOWN HAS FAILED

WHEN COUNTRY PEOPLE COME TO TOWN

When country people come to town, what do they come for?

They come for various things. Most of all, perhaps, to trade—to sell something, or to buy something, or to do both. Or they come on other business errands—to deposit money at the bank or to borrow money there, to pay their taxes, to have a tooth pulled. Or they may come for amusement, or recreation, or uplift—to see the movies or the ball game, to go to a political meeting or to church. They may come on purely social errands—to visit their people in town, or to see other folks from the country, or to attend the lodge or the club.

The average country person has a lot of business in town; not as much business, not as many real reasons for coming to town, as many country persons imagine, but still plenty to bring him often. The town is the country's natural gathering place, as pointed out in an earlier chapter; and the town's welfare depends on the coming to town, with the products they have to sell and the money they have to spend, of all the country folks about it. A lot of the countryman's prosperity or comfort may depend, too, on the way he is treated or the way he feels when he comes to town.

What provision has the average country town made for the convenience or the pleasure of the countryman when he comes inside its borders? What does it do to make his stay while there comfortable and profitable for him?

Not much, it must be admitted. Even less, in most cases, for the farmer's wife and children than for himself.

There has been a great change these latter years in this respect. I can remember when a "ladies' rest room" in a small town was an exceptional institution indeed. Many towns yet lack even this simplest of provisions for its visitors. Many others have "rest rooms" in which no country woman would think of resting if she could find any other place to go. It would be rash even now to say that this very elementary provision for the comfort of the folks who keep the town running has had a fair amount of attention. Still, there has been great progress.

There are libraries in some towns into which the unhurried visitor may turn to spend an unoccupied half-hour; but in many towns there is either no library, or else a library into which no tired woman or weary boy from the country would ever think of going. Our Protestant churches are remarkable for their week-day inhospitality. A strange boy trying to find a resting place about a church on a week day would likely be set upon by the town policeman. Churches may open their doors to all comers for a few hours on Sunday, but they close those doors tightly the rest of the time, and they certainly do not invite strangers to linger in, or around, them "for meditation or for prayer." Some banks and some stores make an effort to provide comfort and a feeling of freedom for their customers when those customers are not transacting business; but these banks and stores are exceptional in the country town. The out-of-town customer is expected to get his business done and to pass on.

Going to town is not so serious a matter for country people as it once was. It does not take them as long, does not entail upon them as much waiting about as it once did. They come less often in the farm wagon, oftener in the Ford—not always a happy sign, but on the whole a desirable development.

But even this change has brought with it troubles to the town-goer. There used to be a generally recognized place for the farmer's wagon to stand or his horses to be hitched. It might not be a convenient place to get at, and he might have to wade dust or mud, according to the season, to get into or out of it, but usually it was there. Strangely, however, some of the very towns that recognized the need of a hitching yard have not yet recognized the need of parking accommodations for the farmer coming to town to trade or to visit. Rural complaint about town speed laws and driving regulations and parking restrictions is frequent. Some towns are still infested with fee-grabbing peace officers whose idea is to get something out of the stranger who comes to town rather than to make his visit a pleasant one. One of the minor, but extremely annoying, pests of our civilization is the peace officer who is looking for a chance to get some one fined or to show his authority, rather than for a chance to be of service. The town with a police officer or two habitually discourteous toward folks from "the sticks" is all the time getting some extremely undesirable advertising.

When country folks come to town they ought to be assured of a good place to leave their cars or their teams; they ought to have a pleasant place to rest or to eat their luncheon, if they should wish to rest or eat; they ought to think of the city officials as friends ready to help them; they ought to expect, in short, a welcome from the town, even while they are not in the act of spending money.

Some farmers will tell one that "plain country people" are not wanted in some town churches. Of that, one not a member of one of the accused churches should be hesitant to judge. Lodges are proverbial places of good fellowship; but public schools are something else in many cases. The country child is not always made to feel welcome in the town school. Sometimes his parents are not encouraged to send him, not even when that is his natural place to go.

Parenthetically, since the paragraph above was written I have had a letter illustrative of this feeling and also of the feeling of inter-town jealousy, of which something will be said in a later chapter. The writer of this letter is the father of one of a little group of country children who have reached high school age. There are two small towns in his county and he writes that "there is feeling between them." He lives near one of them, and there is no other high school in that end of the county. The town charges a high rate of tuition for pupils coming from the outside, and insists on payment in advance each month. The county superintendent of schools lives in the other town, the county seat, and does not like to transfer money from the county school fund to the town in which these children go to school. Last year the money to which these children were entitled was not credited to them until nearly the close of the school year, while the parents had to dig down in their pockets each month to pay tuition for them. This may seem a small matter to the person to whom a few dollars each month is nothing to worry about. Some of these farmers are not in that shape; it is a burden to them to have to meet this extra expense in the schooling of their children. And it is not hard to imagine how little the whole business inclines them to love either town— the one that makes them pay more than they think they should pay, and the one that is willing to hurt them just to show its feeling against the other. This may not be a typical case, but it is not altogether without parallel.

In a word, the town as an institution is not always exactly cordial toward the countryman in town; it is often not very considerate of either his welfare or his comfort; at times, it is to be feared, it forgets to be courteous to him, and forgetting to be courteous, it is in danger of forgetting to be just.

WHEN TOWN PEOPLE GO TO THE COUNTRY

When John Jones and his family go out from Centerville to visit their friends the Browns in the country, the two families conduct themselves toward each other just about as any other two friendly families would conduct themselves. But when the Jones family and the Clark family and the rest of the town folks just go out into the country—auto riding on Sunday afternoon, let us say, or for a hunting or picnicking expedition—they do not always conduct themselves in a way to win the approbation of the Browns and the Greens and the Grays and the other farm families. They are too likely to assume a lot of things no countryman could safely assume in town, and to regard as rights things they should think of as privileges or ask for as favors.

A bit of personal experience may help make this point clear. I have a small country place some little way out of a city. There is a grove on it and a spring, a good place for picnicking. Groups of young people, and older ones, used to come frequently and proceed to disport themselves with much freedom, although this grove and spring are in enclosed grounds and near my house. They come occasionally even now, despite the attempts of some years to impress on all comers that those grounds are not open to the public. To get to this place, these parties have to come through the fields of other landowners and to cross several fences. I take it that they come across all these fields without permission, for I do not recall that a single group ever asked permission of me before spreading its dinner or starting a fire. I am certain that numbers of these people, because of my insistence that they must find some other place to enjoy themselves, have regarded me as a selfish and cantankerous old curmudgeon. They could see no reason why they should not burn my wood and litter up my fields and have a noisily good time for half a day—or half a night—in a "field." The fact that their shouting and laughter might keep us all awake did not affect their point of view at all. They were in the country, and for that reason never thought of themselves as trespassers or as intruders on family privacy. Yet, if I should go into one of their front yards, or back yards, to eat lunch and sing songs, they would probably call the police. They would not themselves think of taking such a liberty with the grounds of their neighbors.

Complaint of this sort is general. Perhaps it is loudest in the vicinity of large cities, but it can be heard around almost any town. Too many towns-folk, when they go to the country, assume an air of superiority or forget that the countryman has and cherishes his individual rights and traditions. The stories of robbed orchards, of broken fences, of front yards plundered of blossoms, are nowhere unusual. Depredations of this type are attributed generally to the hoodlum element, and probably with justice; but sober and influential business men and their families offend in similar, if in not quite as gross, manner. People who pride themselves on their respectability go hunting through the farmer's fields without his permission, litter up his roadsides with cans and bottles and old papers, cut Christmas trees or break down the dogwood bushes along his fence-rows, drive carelessly over his ducks and chickens, and never imagine that they are losing their respectability in a domineering discourtesy or a petty sort of dishonesty.

It is not even implied, of course, that all people from town forget to be courteous and considerate when they go to the country. Most of them do not; friendliness and mutual regard are the rule. Yet the exceptions to this rule are entirely too numerous and too glaring for country folk not to notice them and to feel the sting of them. The towns have failed fully to live up to the Golden Rule, or even to the recognized rules of civilized intercourse; and they owe it to themselves, no less than to the country, to make effective a finer code of manners and morals for the town visitor to the country.

CUSTOMERS OR FELLOW CITIZENS?

Getting down to the essentials of it, one is forced to conclude that the failure of the town to be either a gracious host of the countrymen or graceful visitor to the country is to be traced to a fundamental misconception of the countryman's real relation to the town.

One reading the periodicals of the day finds himself persuaded at times that this is the age of selling. Not in advertising and business journals only, but in the staid magazines, in the daily papers, in the church organs even, he can see at any time where somebody is deeply interested in "selling" something—it may be an idea, or a thought, or a desire, just as well as a machine or a piece of goods—to somebody else, or where some overpowered individual has been happily "sold" on this piece of merchandise or that conception of public duty. Half the country is giving most of its time and thought, one would glean, to the attempt to sell something to the other half. Salesmanship has come to rank not only as a fine art, but in some cases, apparently, as the chief end of man; and the most energetic and demonstrative of all salesmen are to be found among the active spirits of our town organizations. For what do our Chambers of Commerce, and Rotary Clubs, and Kiwanis Clubs, and the rest of these organizations exist but to sell things?

"Sell our town to the farmers," "Sell this idea of coöperation," "Sell your ideals of citizenship to others,"—we have all heard such expressions time and again.

Now, when a man exists, or works, chiefly to sell something, he is likely to think of other folks, first of all, as possible customers. His interest in them is likely to be proportionate to their ability to buy what he has to sell, or to their likelihood of buying. This idea of relationship, it is to be feared, has been developed to such an extent that it has come to color the town's whole view of the countryman. He is thought of primarily not as a fellow citizen or a fellow business man, but as a possible customer, a buyer of goods or ideas the town wishes to send out into the country.

Not all of this desire of the town to sell something to the country is a selfish desire. Of late especially, the towns have gone about selling ideas and ideals, as well as goods and services, to the country. Some of these ideas and ideals have been good ones, too, fine ones; so good and so fine that the attempt to sell them was a pity. They should have been given—should have been presented as matters for mutual consideration and mutual utilization. For the idea of selling is essentially the idea of one mind's overcoming and possessing another mind. Always the seller seeks to lead, to dominate, to bring the buyer to the conclusion that the seller is right. And many a commendable attempt at co-operation has failed because one party took to the other something of his own, intent merely upon winning the second party to an acceptance of it. The true co-operation thinks of the other party as a partner with whom the thing is to be talked over that a mutually satisfactory policy may be agreed on. Salesmanship has its place, but so has co-operation; and the town— ahead of the country as it is in many ways—needs less to sell town ideas and policies and programs to the country than to join with the country in working out policies and programs for both. Many a well-inspired effort at country betterment by a town or a group of townsmen has failed because it was the effort of salesmen rather than of co-operators.

INEFFECTIVE ATTEMPTS AT CO-OPERATION

It has been "quite the thing" of late years for town Chambers of Commerce to invite farmers to become members. In some cases farmers are received at nominal fees, and are sought often in wholesale lots. This well-meant effort at co-operation has done something toward bringing about a better understanding between town and country; but it has seldom produced any notable results. Such results could scarcely be expected of it. It has had in it too little of understanding.

A member of one of these small town Chambers of Commerce, a man who is at once a farmer and a successful business man, gave the reason for the comparative failure of most of these efforts in some very plain language. He was telling me what he had told his own Chamber of Commerce when it was proposed to go out into the farming sections for members:

"You won't get anywhere with this plan for several reasons. In the first place, this is a town organization; it exists to look after the interests of G and to help work out its problems. Most of the problems it has to work out are purely town problems. These are the things you think most about and give most attention to. You think of it as a town organization, and so do the farmers.

"For this reason many farmers will not care to join it. If you get them in at a cheaper rate than the rest of us have to pay, they will not feel like they are regularly a part of the organization, and neither will you. Most of you will expect them to discuss only matters of town-and-country interest, to be a sort of visiting representation. They will not feel at home here. Most of them will not come at all, and the few who do come will not likely come often or feel like taking a very active part. You wouldn't either, in their place.

"If you want to meet the farmers as man to man and talk over the things all of you are interested in, get up a special town-and-country organization, or appoint a committee of this organization to meet with a committee from the Farm Bureau, and let those committees meet on an equal footing and work out a program for all of us."

There was sense in what this man said. Not that it is bad for farmers to belong to town organizations or for townsmen to belong to farmer organizations. Both of these are all right—as far as they go. They help to promote goodwill and understanding. But they do not go far enough; they are inadequate to any lasting accomplishment because they do not bring the two sets of men together on a basis of equality. And that is a thing needed where real results are to be sought for.

Some Chambers of Commerce have sought to lay the foundation for concerted action by changing themselves bodily from town to town-and-country organizations. This is a courageous tackling of the difficulty. It may overcome it in some cases. It shows, at least, an understanding of the situation, an insight into the spiritual processes required to bridge over the needless division. Yet there is danger that the new county Chamber of Commerce may remain the old town organization under a new name, or—a smaller danger—that it may become but a modified form of farm organization. Besides, it is to be recognized that there will remain some distinction, some conflict even, between town and country interests. The strictly farmer organization will still be needed, as will the purely town organization. It is a mistake for a Farm Bureau or a farmers' co-operative to get too many townsmen in it; to get too much of the town point of view. Despite all I have said about the desirability of town and country co-operation and about the mutuality of town and country interests, I am persuaded that even the small town will be benefited by having its leaders of thought and action get together simply as townsmen and discuss the town and its needs. When the farmers have worked out their policies and programs, and when the townsmen have done the same, they will both be ready to get together to work out whatever may be called for in the way of compromise, of accommodation, of adjustment, and of active co-operation.

Every effort of the country town to co-operate with the country about it or to draw the farmer folk about it closer to it in feeling and action is to be commended. Many such efforts, however, have failed, or amounted to little, chiefly because they were made with the idea that the farmer could be induced to come into a town band and play second fiddle, or rattle the bones. The effort to get him to do this much, the willingness to give him even this place, may indicate an increasing understanding or neighborliness, but they fall short of the real co-operation that must be had to make the joint efforts of town and country fruitful and profitable.

Speaking generally and at large, the towns have failed in their efforts to bring about town and country co-operation; and they have failed chiefly because they were interested in selling the farmer something for their own profit, or in doing some sort of missionary work to uplift and advance him. The farmer is, as a rule, shrewd enough to detect the former purpose, and he is usually sufficiently self-reliant or stubborn to resent the latter. But he will nearly always respond to the advances of his town when it meets him on an equal footing and, with an outstretched hand of respecting friendliness, stands ready to talk things over with him and to seek for common understandings and policies of mutual benefit.

THE MAIN STREET POINT OF VIEW

Any failure of any attempt of any town to co-operate profitably with its surrounding country is a commendable failure, however; the great failure of the towns has been their failure to think of the country in connection with their own future. The worst thing that ails our American country towns, as I have more than once intimated, is their myopia, their proneness to see only to the end of Main Street, and to think that a town grows of itself and from its stores and shops outward. A city has the Main Street point of view when it looks down from the height of its own size to sneer at or to feel sorry for the little town with but one important thoroughfare; a town has the Main Street point of view when it thinks of its one important thoroughfare as a road to the city instead of a way to the country. And many a little town has this point of view. Cure the country towns of this defect of vision and understanding, and both material and spiritual development beyond the dreams of most town dwellers becomes possible for them.

Chapter IX

WHERE THE TOWN MUST LEAD

Too often in their dealings the folks from town have met the folks from the country with an air of superiority and a disposition to smile at, rather than with, them. And too often the folks from the country have faced the folks from town with that feeling of inferiority which leads to imitation on the one hand and resentment on the other hand.

Townsfolk are in no way essentially better than country folk, but it would be folly to deny that townsfolk are in many ways ahead of country folk. The town leads; it has the new books, the new plays, the new fashions, the new manners, the new ideas, mostly before the country has them. Not all of these new things are improvements over the old—change is not always progress, nor novelty improvement—but the country follows the town and not the town the country. The country belle and beau try to dress like the girls and boys of the town; the country Sunday school will be singing next year the songs the town Sunday school is trying out this year; the town's ideas about education and home decoration and sanitation gradually work themselves out into the farmer mind. The graces and refinements—true or false—that give distinction to social intercourse or "tone" to social "affairs" are urban and not rural; the country looks to the town to find out about these things.

This is but the natural, the inevitable result of the greater concentration of wealth in the town. Culture and grace and refinement, attention to the finer manners and customs, appreciation of beauty and the esthetic side of life wait for their development on the establishment of a leisure class, of groups of people with minds and bodies sufficiently unoccupied by the making of a living to find pleasure in, and to give time and thought to, the things that do not help to preserve life, but only help to enjoy it. In even the small town will be found some few persons who really belong to the leisure class. And these few persons—wives and daughters of men who have made more money than their neighbors, a few young men as yet unbroken to or unplaced in the business scheme of things, a few older men retired from active labor—will by the very force of circumstances become that town's social leaders. The society they form will likely be formed after what they know of the society of larger cities; and it may be in reality a better or a worse society than the town has had before, but to its manners and customs and standards the rest of the town will tend to conform. And to the manners and customs and standards of the town the country about the town will all the time tend, more or less closely, to conform.

There may be something to deplore in all this; it may be that it would be better for the country to be more independent in some of its ways—for its women, for example, to make their Sunday clothes more to fit country conditions and less to resemble prevailing fashions brought from distant cities; for its dinners and parties to cling more closely to rural tradition and to follow less after city customs; for its schools and churches, its habits of speech and deportment to develop less after those of the centers of population; but however this may be, it is certain that the country profits in many ways by going to school to the town and by following its example. For, however lightly the town may seem at times to regard literature, or music, or science, or the art of fine living, certain it is that of all these it has more than the country. With much that it could well do without, no doubt, the country certainly gets from the town much that it sorely needs.

The town has larger possession than the country of the graces and refinements and niceties of life, and the country but recognizes a fact when it looks to the town for these things.

A SOCIAL AND AN EDUCATIONAL CENTER

The town, then, is able to be—is almost of necessity—a social and educational center for the country about it. It is in position to make the social life of the country about it a fairer and finer thing than it would be if the country were left to its own devices. It is in line to carry from the great centers of human thought and activity the best of literature, of music, of drama, of painting and sculpture and architecture even, out to where every farm family may come into touch with them.

I am not saying, of course, that any country town can provide for its rural neighbors, or for itself, all of the best of literature or of music or of art. The country town's circulating library may have to get along with a score or two of new books in a year, and may have to resist pressure to keep all these from being popular novels. It may have to let its band play just such pieces as that band can play and get its opera in snatches on the victrola or from the radio. It may see no drama outside of the "movie palaces." It may see great painting and sculpture only in black and white reproductions, and it may have to guard itself against delirium tremens whenever it looks long and earnestly at its own business fronts and civic structures; but whatever its limitations may be—and they grow smaller all the time—it is within touch of the world's activities and is in a better position than the country to seek and to find out, to enjoy and to pass on what is good.

The town feels, subconsciously often, this advantage it has, and so does the country. It is doubtful if either of them often faces the fact of it with clear thought of its meaning to both. If the town did this, there would be less of snobbishness and more of helpfulness in its social dealings with the country; if the country did it, there would be less of both injudicious imitation and censorious criticism. The influence of the town here may be an impalpable thing, but it is a very real thing, and its responsibility to pass on to the rural communities the best of what comes to it is a very real responsibility.

OTHER THINGS IN WHICH THE TOWN LEADS

It is not only in the development of a finer social life that the town leads the country. It is, by force of circumstances, in advance of the country in various other ways.

Take, for example, the matter of sanitation and health protection, to which reference has been made. The very fact of the town's existence—the crowding together of numerous people—forces it to take an interest in this matter which the country can get along without. The farmer may dump garbage out in his back yard and human refuse in a neighboring gulley and get away with it for a long time. The townsman simply cannot do this. He comes shortly to see the necessity of some sanitary precautions, and from his own necessity and his own experience he is likely to see before the countryman does the necessity of some sanitary precautions in the country. He realizes the danger of the unprotected water source, the carelessly handled milk supply, before the countryman does, simply because his conditions have given him a bit of education along these lines the countryman has not had. Consequently, it is he and not the countryman who will move for slaughter house regulation, for dairy inspection, for an adequate public health service. And when he moves for these things, he will find more often than not a good part of the country in opposition to him. He is asking the country to change its habits and its customs for reasons which he understands and the country does not. The temptation in such case to feel both

superior and resentful is a great one. He is but too
apt to think of the countryman as both an ignoramus
who does not desire enlightenment and a stubbornly
stupid fellow who needs to be run over for his own
good.

So it is that often in his fight for advancement of
one kind or another the townsman is right in his
choosing of a side and wrong in his methods of
combat. Better schools, better roads, better health
service are time and again given by the town to the
countryman against his will; and the town is to be
commended for the gift; but always it is even more
important to change the country outlook and the
country will than to change its conditions. The wise
townsman who would give the country better things
will think first of all of giving it the wider outlook,
the more progressive point of view. It is hard to push
any people along the road to progress; and pushing
should be resorted to only as a last hope.

Perhaps as good an example as can be found where
the town has been mostly right in its purposes and
mostly wrong in its methods is in the game laws.
The movement for game protection has come largely
from the cities and towns. In many country districts
—most of them possibly—it has met with little support. The countryman will tell one that he believes
the game should be protected and the laws for its
protection should be enforced; but the chances are
that he will like least of all the town organizations
and the town sportsmen chiefly responsible for the
laws and their enforcement. Usually, too, he will have

good reason for his dislikes. For most game laws
have been primarily for the protection of a certain
class of sportsmen and have failed to protect the
landowner on whose premises the game is to be
found. "We raise the game and the sports from town
kill it," I have heard farmers say; and their complaint had justification. The farmer will have been
used to going out when he feels like it and shooting
the birds and squirrels in his own fields and woods,
and if he wishes, going on over to his neighbor's
fields and woods. Neither he nor his neighbor, probably, will spend much time hunting. Both of them will
resent it when told that they must take out a hunter's
license if they are to step off their own land with a
gun; and both of them will resent the coming of
hunters from town who will take their licenses as
authority to wander where they please, shooting at
what they like. In most cases the farmer, to protect
his fields from intrusion of undesired hunters, is
obliged to "post" them or otherwise serve formal
notice that trespassing on them is not desired. This is
manifestly unjust; the hunter should be the man required to make sure of his ways, since he is going
out to enjoy himself on people's property and to enjoy himself with a possession of the State produced
at the expense—if there be an expense—of the landowner. Even when the law requires that the hunter
obtain permission before going on a farmer's land,
the farmer is at a disadvantage. Few men have either
the time or the disposition to chase down a trespassing hunter, learn his name or his number, report or

bring action against him, or go through all the fuss and worry necessary to protect themselves.

It is not strange that there is so much rural feeling against game laws and game shooters. Yet game laws are necessary, and left to themselves it is to be feared that the farmers would let the game of the country be practically wiped out before taking measures for its protection. The townsmen who have moved for its protection have been right; they have been in advance of the countryman in their perception of the country's needs in the case; but they have none the less been unjust to the farmer in many cases, both in the laws made and in the practices followed. Satisfactory and just game protection will be had only when the country is given a voice in the making of the system.

SAVING THE COUNTRY FROM ITSELF

The greatest fault of the countryside, probably the greatest hindrance to its progress, is its too great conservatism. The country is more conservative than the town in almost every way—even politically. Political progress when one looks into the matter, will be found to come mostly from the cities. The political radicalism of Northwestern farmers is a very intermittent radicalism. Normally, these farmers are conservative. It is only in times of distress or reaction that they go radical. There was a very definite economic reason for the Populist party, and an equally obvious one for the Non-partisan League. The conditions that caused these outbreaks partially removed, the masses of those farmers turned back to vote for McKinley and for Coolidge. Besides, most of the proposals of these so-called radicals had been made many times before, and few of them, analyzed, were so very radical after all. It is to be remembered, too, that what may seem a great change to one part of this country may seem to another part of it but a clinging to old institutions or old traditions.

But political analyses need not concern us here. The country is essentially conservative as compared with the city. It is conservative in its ways, its customs, its habits of thought, its methods of life. Old books and old creeds hold their influence longest in the country. Continuously the country's population sorts itself out, the progressive part of it moving away, the conservative part staying at home.

Conservatism is a good thing; so is radicalism. It has been well said that the radical is the engine of, the conservative the brakes on, the car of progress. Without the engine—without the new ideas of the radical—the advance of humanity would stop and the rust of disuse consume the car of civilization. Without the brakes—without the doubts and the inertia that make great changes slow and difficult—society would smash itself to pieces on the rocks of reckless experiment.

The country is not without leadership of its own. It is going, let us believe, to develop more leaders and more far-seeing leaders in the future. It is all the time, too, furnishing leaders for the town. But all the time the country needs leadership in one way or another from the town. The town banker may be a mighty force in improving farming methods in his county. The town teacher may be just the man to introduce a needed change to country schools, the town preacher may well set a higher standard for country sermons, the town society leader is in a position to add brightness and refinement to the social life of the country.

In this respect, the town must be active to save the country from itself, from its own too great conservatism. If town and country are to progress together, the best leadership of the town has a mission in the country. But here the warning once given may well be repeated. The country needs leadership from the town, the leadership of practical example as well as of wholesome precept; but it does not need condescension or coercion. The country is to develop along with the town, but it is not to develop into the town or into an imitation of it. Country traditions are not always things to direct life by, but they are usually things to be respected, and for them there are usually reasons it is well to ascertain. The leadership that would condemn in the country everything that departs from town standards is a leadership that will not lead far. The country school may learn from the town school; but the country school needs to remain —probably more often to become—different from the town school. So does the country church, the country club, the country business organization. So does the social organization of the country; a country party, a country dinner, should not be like a town party, a town dinner. Both may be more refined, more satisfying, if their givers have been to town parties and town dinners; but either will be flat and unprofitable if it is but an imitation of something planned for different people under different conditions.

The town is in advance of the country in numerous ways; it has much to give the country in the way of leading and enlightenment. It can give the most fully, however, can make its leadership the most effective, only when it gives to the country, along with what is best of its own attainments, appreciation of and pride in the best of the old country traditions and customs and graces.

Chapter X

THE SOUL OF THE TOWN

MAIN STREET AGAIN

Regardless of whether Sinclair Lewis's *Main Street* is a great novel or merely a clever one, it struck home to the thought and feeling of a nation as no other novel of a generation has done. People felt it. Not only did its title become an everyday phrase and a phrase with a real meaning in it, but people looked at the small town in the book, recognized it as their own town, and saw, perhaps, that town in a truer light than they had ever before seen it. The book's success, its appeal, came not from the frequently unconvincing Carol Kennicott, but from the absolutely convincing citizens and sentiments of Gopher Prairie. Main Street runs through nearly every county seat; its four squares, or one, or a dozen, of "business buildings" are known to all of us. In any town of a few hundred or a few thousand people Sam Clark lives, and Uncle Whittier, and Juanita Haydock, and Mrs. Bogart. And because they are so numerous and so essentially a part of the town life, the town's thoughts become even as theirs.

To be sure, the picture of the American small town in the book is not a complete picture. Photographic though it is in its reality, it is a photograph made from the town's unattractive side. For the typical small town is not altogether smug and stupid

[138]

and trivial and uncharitable, ugly of body and little
of soul. It has all of these defects in abounding,
often in excessive, measure; but it has also much of
worthy aspiration, of wholesome self-respect, of out-
reaching kindness. As in the soul of the average
individual, good and evil exist side by side; so in
the soul of the average town. It is but common sense
to face the fact that most towns lack the inspiration
of a definite purpose or of a high ideal, that they are
generally trying to fashion themselves into imitations
of other towns, but it is only just and sensible to face
the other fact that every little town hides in itself
unmeasured potentialities of development.

The trouble is not that the town, despite the self-
complacency it so often displays, does not wish to be
something more than it is; but that it has, usually, so
little originality in its conception of what it could or
would like to be,

    "City-making villages

      Small towns that yet refused to be themselves,

      But tried to ape the city and its ways"—

as Charles Divine puts it. Rare indeed is the town
without ambition; equally rare the town with any
definite ambition—except to be bigger—or any conception of itself as an individuality ministering to a
definite section of country, a particular body of people, and so privileged to develop itself along individual lines into the dignity of a self-satisfying and
self-justifying independence and uniqueness.

"God made the country and man made the town,"

said the poet; and the wag amended the saying to, "God made the country, man the city, and the devil the small town." Few, probably, have lived in a small town without at times feeling that the gibe had justification; and that in the town, lacking both country independence and city freedom, life is cramped by the petty tyranny of a narrow public opinion and the constant pressure of an intrusive neighborliness as nowhere else in the world. Few, too, but have felt at one time or another that the town itself was the last word in futility, forever seeking to justify itself to itself; and yet forever seeking to be something other than itself. Yet, for these disadvantages of small town life there are—at least there might be—abundant compensations. The small town might be almost the best place in all the world to live. Few readers, probably, but have pictured to themselves a town bringing to itself the best of country life to join with the best of city life. Give almost any country town a wholesome ideal for itself, set for it a worthy goal toward which to strive, and in it men and women could scarcely fail to find opportunity for continued and useful effort and for continuous and effective self-expression.

Our little towns lack beauty and dignity and serenity of soul more because they lack the inspiration of attainable ideals, or because they have too mistaken ideals, than for any other reason. A town, like a man, must know what it wishes to be before it can realize itself.

THE OBSESSION OF BIGNESS

Many towns, unfortunately, know exactly what they wish to become—they wish to become cities, and spend their thought and effort on the acquiring of bigness. Much of the town's failure, where it has failed, is directly due to this mistaken ideal, this sad misunderstanding of itself. Some towns grow into cities; most do not and should not. The country town is not merely the embryo of, or the foundation work for, a city. It is something far different, a living, purposeful, self-contained individuality that has no cause to grow out of itself into something else. Long ago, Plutarch, who was a wise man in his day, wrote of the call to the great cities.

"But for me, I live in a little town, where I am willing to continue, lest it grow less."

Plutarch was a good citizen; it is safe to say that he had the friendship and respect of his neighbors. The man who loves his town is likely to be loved of his townsmen. The man who would have his shortcomings charged to himself, and not to his obscure birthplace or provincial residence, could not but have been a man of influence in local affairs— the sort of man to whom the neighbors would go for advice and assistance, equally confident of his sanity and good will.

Still, if Plutarch lived today, much as most of us might value him as a neighbor, we might secretly look upon him as rather old-fogyish and out of date.

Remain in a small town for fear it should become

smaller? Not we. If it is not going to get bigger, let us go to some town that will.

Most of us still think of the town as a place that is going to be a city. The obsession of bigness is upon us. Urbetta wants new mills and machine shops that it may rival Greattown in population and bank clearings. Bigburg wants a new opera house and a street car line down the two main streets, so that it can get in the Urbetta class. Littleville lays off new streets and sells good farm lands at unreasonable prices, hoping in this way to start a "boom" and catch up with Bigburg. And out at the Cross Roads, where half a dozen little houses have been put up near the church and the store and the blacksmith shop to catch and hold for a few months at a time a few families of the more transient and laboring class—out there in the sun-quickened and wind-refreshed fields, the building of another inconvenient, unsightly house to rent to some unknown straggler is regarded hopefully as another step toward the blissful goal of real townhood.

Yet, what has the number of people in any of these places to do with its desirability as a place for men to live and work, and for children to be born and grow up in?

Does Urbetta really need new manufacturing plants, new rows of squalid "mill-hand" houses, new supplies of smoke and dust and grime, when it thrives on its trade with the surrounding country and has unimproved and unsuspected beauty spots all along the banks of the little river where the big mills "ought to be"?

Has it ever occurred to Bigburg that it would add more to that place's charm and fragrance to move the pig-pens out of town, to fill up the mud-holes where the "streets" dwindle down into country roads, and to pull down the ram-shackle old firetrap across from the depot, than to build an opera house or street car line with the prospect of seeing the builder get two per cent on his money?

And Littleville, where each family has, from either front or back yard, a fine view of a wooded cliff, and where all wade through mud in wet weather and kick up dust in dry weather as they go to church or to post-office—can not Littleville realize that what it needs is to put down a few rods of concrete walk and to make sure that the trees on the cliff will not be cut? The fields can grow grass and grain and help pay for the walks, if they are left as fields; cut up into town lots, they will grow up in weeds, most likely, and yield no return.

And our Cross Roads friends, why do they want more children of uncertain ancestry and unpatched trousers in their schools; more ugly little houses to mar the beauty of the pastures? Can't they see that what the Cross Roads needs is a coat of paint on the "storehouse," and some vines and hedges to screen some of the unkempt-looking outhouses?

Suggest these things to the people of these towns— tell them to make a park of the river bank, to get rid of the mudholes, to put down the new walks—and they will tell you in all seriousness that they have not the money, that taxes are too high now, and that what the place needs is new settlers and new enterprises.

And yet the little city will buy a site by the river and give it to some corporation, if the corporation can only be induced to build its new mill there instead of elsewhere. There will be big meetings, too, to start that new street car line that is not needed and cannot pay. And if Littleville has a struggling newspaper, that paper will print long accounts of the big sale of lots and the "phenomenal growth of our young city," with never a word about the beauty of the green-clad cliff, or the needlessness of the mud-spattered shoes.

The question with the town is not "How good?" but "How big?"

There must come another point of view. The little city must come to wish other things more than to be a big city next year; the country town must cease aspiring to be a city at all; the little hamlet must lose its desire to push the wheat fields back from its doors. Instead, the citizens of all of them must begin to dream the dream of the town that ought to be, and begin to labor that this dream may come to pass. For surely, it is more important that the town be beautiful and clean and well-governed than that it be big; and just as surely will present cult of numbers pass away and the more rational appreciation of homelikeness and wholesome surroundings take its place in the minds of the people who dwell in our American towns.

Taken in its entirety, the town of today, big or little, is an unlovely thing. Exceptions there may be, but the rule holds good. In almost every town, too, may be found beauty spots—fine residence sections where trees border the curving avenues and the lawns are kept green; public buildings, not faultless, perhaps, but sufficiently dignified and purposeful to give the citizens a feeling of pride; smooth, well-lighted streets, well designed and fitting business houses. There are few even of the smaller towns which have not some feature either of natural beauty or civic achievement which they are proud to possess and glad to see each day. Even the tall smokestacks of the mills, waving the dark plumes of industry above roof and spire, and the grim-fronted furnaces which brighten now and then with the unexpected and thrilling splendor of leaping flame and billowing vapor, crimson and purple and rose and turquoise and tender gray—even these utilitarian structures have their charm. The town is not devoid of beauty; but how seldom it can be said to be beautiful!

Against the better residence districts, clean, fair-fronted, must be placed the slum districts or the negro quarters with their dismal grouping of poverty and squalor. Against the stately buildings may be placed the ramshackle old structures which are allowed to stand, often menacing as well as unsightly. Against the strength and majesty of mill and furnace, the wretched cheapness and slatternly monotony of the long rows of houses, all alike, in which the men who work in the mill and furnace are expected to live, as if a laborer had no sense of beauty or no aspiration for the finer things of life.

But why continue the list? We all know these defects of our towns—the squalor and the filth that even villages manage to accumulate and shelter; the ragged, unkempt district that so often both joins and separates town and country. We have seen them, and a thousand other unlovely sights, so often that we have come complacently to accept them as part of the natural order of things; or else have imagined that the way to get rid of them is to "boost the town" and have it grow. If only people would come in and land go up and a few men grow rich because of that, all would be well, and we need not concern ourselves about the noble trees that were cut down, the clear springs that became defiled, or the poorer families that were crowded into less and less desirable homes.

We shall yet come to think of another type of town with a finer and higher ideal—the town that shall be all beautiful, that desires more inhabitants less than it desires better and happier citizens—and when we have come to think of and to long for it, somewhere in splendid palpable reality, built by the cheerful toil of men who love their homes, and firm-planted on rocky hillside or billowing prairie with which it recognizes kinship, this town will come into being.

"A city is not builded in a day;" and we need not

expect to see our ideal town spring suddenly into
existence. The passion for virtue and beauty and
sanity of life is not going to possess any existing
county seat and convert it into the village of our
dreams. There is no Merlin of industry to build for
us a modern Camelot. It is only by gradual processes
that our little town will come to recognize its kinship
with the fields and deliberately set itself the mission
of living not only among them but with them, of
having their atmosphere flow through its streets and
of extending its modernities out into their lanes until
town and country become but parts of a single well-
defined and well-organized whole.

Something like this, it seems to me, must come to
pass. Slowly, no doubt, as the growth of trees in the
forest or the city street, but none the less surely and
irrevocably, the little town will come into its own.
Some day this town will show itself not as a means,
but as an end, and plan to become the right sort of
town instead of longing to become any sort of city.

And in this town, beyond all question, life will be
better ordered, more purposeful, and fuller of "dur-
able satisfaction" than is the town life of today.
There will be no hint of stagnation, no slacking of
enterprise because some rival town has made more
rapid growth. Instead there will be more beauty,
and a deeper and finer local pride. In such towns
Plutarchs may not live; but there will surely be men
of worth and strength—men whom Plutarch would
have been glad to know—and whether or not they
attain distinction beyond their own town, these men

will add distinction to it. With men willing to live in little towns and to serve them, to keep them from growing less, not merely in number, but in beauty, desirability, and friendliness, the future of the nation will be assured.

SMALL TOWN RIVALRIES

Closely allied to, indeed growing out of, this passion for increasing size on the part of the small town is the unworthy jealousy that one town often feels for another. The feeling that if Five Points grows and prospers, the neighboring Four Corners must grow less and prosper less is a common one. It originates almost surely from the idea that to grow and to prosper are the same thing, and that the business of towns is not to get better, but to get bigger; not to become a more desirable place for the people now in them to live, but to get more people to living in them. This small town jealousy is shown in a hundred ways, and nearly always it reacts harmfully upon all the towns involved.

I have mentioned the case of the hydro-electric plants at L and C. One of C's reasons for refusing to sell power and to make a profit out of it had been the fear that a neighboring little village or two would draw on that power and grow by its aid. I have referred also to the case of the two towns in the one county which could not agree about their high school appropriations, because one town was not willing to see the other get ahead of it. The farmers about one town suffered because of this inter-town quarrel; probably both towns lost by it. It is hard to see how anybody could gain by it. One more example coming under my notice may be mentioned—a quarrel between two little hamlets, mere country trading stations.

In a beautiful valley, rich in natural resources and in historic association, even though still suffering from the effects of a one-sided and short-sighted system of farming, are two little towns, mere burgs, about two miles apart. One of them is a very old town; a half dozen houses, built long ago for rich planters and still bearing traces of their old-time grandeur, are its dominating features. Its people are largely descendants of those early day planters and still keep up, to a large degree, the traditions of the old aristocracy. The town was old when the railroad was built through the valley, and the railroad has been there many years.

The old town was disappointed when the railroad was put off to one side of it, and it has never been quite able to forgive the new village that sprang up by the railway to be the neighborhood's gateway to the rest of the world. Always when it has come to a show down, the two towns have been rivals and antagonists.

The road through this part of the valley is a rather bad road. It is fairly good when the weather is good, but when the rains come and the clay softens into mud, and the big river backs up into the creek across which the citizens of both towns must pass to get out, the road is sorry enough.

That creek is a trouble maker. Some years ago, the

county voted money to build concrete bridges over it. A road runs directly from the Old Town across the creek to the section's trading center beyond; the New Town folks go another way.

Naturally the citizens of the Old Town wished the new bridge built on their own road. But a New Town resident was in a position of some authority just then and he and some of the Old Town people were not on the best of terms. So the bridge was built on a sort of cut-off road between the two places, a road on which there was comparatively little travel and which was a mile or two out of the way for the Old Towners. Naturally, the bad feeling between the two towns was intensified.

Lately the people of both villages decided that it was time to build a real road out and to quit staying shut in when the weather went wrong. They got together and raised sufficient money to match the county appropriation that was conditionally made to them. The road building began and a new era of good feeling seemed at hand. It lasted only until the troublesome creek was reached. Then the Old Town people said the road must go by their place, and that a new bridge must be built. The available money was counted and the cost of the bridge was investigated. There was not enough money to build another bridge. "But we will never put a cent into a road that goes away off there and doesn't touch our place," said the Old Towners.

"But you've got a bridge there," retorted the New Towners, "and no money to build another bridge, and we certainly are not going to put our money into a road that will not get us across the creek when it gets up. That old floating bridge of yours is under the water whenever the river rises, and we want a road that will let us out."

Neither side would yield. They fussed about it until the county withdrew its appropriation, and there both towns are—a good road to within two miles of one of them, but between them and the road a gulf of mud and water that keeps them off it and at home when the weather is bad.

The citizens meet each other every day; personally and socially they are neighbors, but as citizens of different towns they cannot agree, and they do not. If they must all suffer because they cannot agree— well, they have been suffering this long time and they feel able to keep it up a while longer.

THE SAVING GRACE OF AN IDEAL

Granting, then, that a town is not merely an embryo city, and that its mission is not merely to gather into itself more dwellings and stores and shops, to lengthen its streets and add new stories to its business blocks; granting that a town does not live and thrive by itself, and that its interests are not antagonistic to the interests of the towns about it; granting, finally, that the chief end of a country town is to serve as the center of business enterprise and social activity for the countryside about it, that it is to be a veritable heart, pumping the life-blood of new labors, new thoughts, new aspirations, through all its channels of trade and intercourse, one comes face to face with the question: How is the town to become this larger community center; how is it to bring itself into closer relationship with the country that is in so many ways a part of it?

If the town is to seek betterness instead of bigness, just how is it to start in that search?

He must be either a very wise man or a very presumptuous man who would attempt to answer these questions definitely and conclusively. It is doubtful if any town will find for itself any full or satisfying answer to either of them. For every individual town, too, an individual answer must be found. The problems of two towns may be similar, but they are not likely to be identical. If any town is to solve the problem of adjustment to the country about it, it must make the experience of other towns a less important factor in its equation than the particular conditions and resources and needs of itself and of the country about.

Most towns have plenty of machinery for town improvement. Some of these machines do little else than make their own wheels go around with more or less clatter, but most of them are capable of being hitched up to tasks worth the doing. The "boosting" organizations of one kind or another are "thick as leaves that strew the banks of Vallombrosa." Chambers of Commerce, Luncheon Clubs, Merchants' Associations, and all the rest—the town without one, at least, of them scarcely feels itself a town at all. And most of them are busily engaged one-half the time in telling the world what a great place The Town is, and the other half the time in trying to devise ways and means of getting more people to come to it to trade or to live. It would seem a not impossible task —though it would seldom be an easy one—to engage an organization of this kind in a serious study of the town and the country about it. Even a booster's club, if it set itself to the task of finding just what the town's shortcomings were and to devising means for their correction, could learn a lot for itself and be in position to teach the town a lot.

Organizations more definitely purposeful—village improvement societies, educational organizations, clubs formed for special purposes—these should be in position to help the town itself, to fix ideals for it, to help it find its soul and give that soul a chance to grow. In most towns some such organization has helped, or is helping now, to do these things; but usually they, too, have lacked the larger vision, have thought of the town as ending with the corporate limits and of the fields and woods beyond as alien territory. The things they have done are but the earnest of the things they could do, once the true place of the town in our civilization and its true relation to the country about were grasped.

Not long since I went one evening to the railway station in a little country town to wait for the train. I chanced to be an hour early. An employee came in to turn on the lights in the waiting room and start a fire that soon went out. Then he went his way, and the boys began coming in. I counted sixteen of them altogether, from a dozen years old up to eighteen possibly. One or two of them seemed to have business there; most of them did not. They were simply loafing, "killing time at the depot" because there were other boys there and, evidently, because they had nowhere else to go, nothing else to do. It was interesting to meet there, listen to some of the tougher fellows tell dirty stories and make unclean allusions to various townsfolk—at least, it was more interesting than anything else they had to do. So there they were—drifting in and out, wasting time, encouraging each other to develop their worst traits. This was the meeting place the town had provided for them, the training school it had opened to them. At least, it had offered no others; probably the two or three toughest boys were responsible for this phase of the community life. In any case, here the future citizenship of the town was being trained. That town has many churches and goes to them on Sunday. Much thought is given to the saving of certain individual souls; but the soul of the town seemed to me a matter of slight concern to it. I may have been wrong in that; but I was not wrong in recognizing the boys with the foul tongues as the makers of that town's future. The town had never thought, evidently, of the tremendous waste of young life that nightly goes on about its little depot. There was a job waiting for one of its numerous organizations, and a job that might be worth to it more than a score of stereotyped "advertising campaigns."

The point is that a town, like a child, can be

brought up or just allowed to grow up. So far as its young folks and the young folks of the country about are concerned, this town is trusting too much to chance, too little to forethought and care.

No individual, no group even, is likely to make the town just what it would like to make it—and that is probably well; but any group, any individual, can in somewise affect the development of his town if he but brings a real idea to the town's store of thought. The soul of a town may be as real as the body of that town, and like the body it will be a composite thing, built up of the thoughts and the desires of many men as the body of the town is built up of the dwelling places and working places of many men.

A country town feeling itself the center and the living heart of the territory and the population that comes to it to do business, to find amusement, or to seek instruction, would as surely become a living entity with a living and growing soul, as does the healthy infant grow up into an inquiring and reasoning child.

A FEW POSSIBILITIES

No attempt has been made here, none will be made, to answer fully the questions asked above; and yet I trust that I have not written all these pages without making, or at least suggesting, some partial answers.

That the town may often help the country by welcoming the country to its churches, I have said. It might help in other cases by a systematic lending of its best church talent, ministerial and lay, to country communities that need such help. It might well lend whatever spiritual influences it possesses to the lessening of denominational disputes and rivalries in over-churched country districts. It should not be impossible in many cases to organize what may be called the more secular church activities for the larger district which includes the town and its tributary countryside.

That the town should help the country schools by contributing from its abundance to the financial lack of the poorer country districts, and why it should do so, I have explained at length. In some cases the call on it to preach the need of education and of more interest in the schools is imperative. Out of its usually larger acquisition of knowledge and culture it should contribute educational impetus as well as educational funds to the way-back districts that are content to remain in darkness. Often, too, the town needs to invite the country children to its own schools, to make them welcome there, possibly to modify somewhat some of the features of those schools to make them more serviceable to country children. I write myself down as a believer in country schools rather than town schools, or imitation town schools, for country children; but I know that the one practical high school for great numbers of country children is the high school in the nearby town; and the town with a fully developed soul will think of a school of this wider service as a town- and-country school.

The village improvement club, the town society for the protection of birds, or the improvement of health

conditions, or the study of Shakespeare, or the mark-
ing of historic spots, has literally no business to be
strictly a town organization if there is a country
about the town. The interests of the family on Main
Street and the family on Lonely Lane are identical
when these things are under consideration.

That the town is naturally the social center of the
country about, with the privileges and the responsi-
bilities of leadership for its own, I have said; as also
that while there may well be town customs and country customs, a town society and a country society,
there should be no sharp-drawn line of division between them. Rather they should be as diverging
branches of the same plant, or as leaf and blossom on
the same bough. That town society which cherishes
snobbish aloofness from the sons and daughters of
the farm has not yet grown a soul of much size.

For amusement the country comes to the town
more frequently than ever before. Perhaps it comes
too often in many cases, and would be better off
developing its own amusements for itself. It is good
for man to play as well as to work, we have come
to believe; and certainly play has been made more
varied and more expensive than ever before. Whether or not it has become more joyful, is an open question. It is better usually for a country district to go
to a schoolhouse playground or a farmer's pasture
to watch two farm boy baseball teams play than for
it to go to town to watch two teams of professionals.
Movies in the schoolhouse can come only now and
then; but now and then they are to be preferred to

the more technically satisfying movies in the town
showhouse. Better than even a good movie on occasion is the play staged by the community's own boys
and girls. Better than any radio concert, the annual
neighborhood "singing."

Town and country, America remains poor in
amusements—it has what it can buy, but mostly does
without what it would have to originate and carry
out for itself. When one thinks of what could be
done in almost any country town by the development
of such musical and dramatic talent as the town and
country about it has available, he realizes that here
waits one of the town's greatest opportunities for the
finding of its own soul and for the voicing of that
soul's finest desires and noblest ambitions. Yet community dramatic clubs, town orchestras, county
choruses are strange things and seldom found. When
a country town decides that the people about it need
some amusement other than the movies—or that it
is time to bring a lot of country folks to town to
boom trade—it may stage a pageant of local history,
but it is just as likely to invite a "carnival company"
with all manner of cheap and doubtful "attractions"
to town and, actually if not avowedly, to let the town
run "wide open" for a week.

Of the town's opportunity to identify itself more
closely with the country in business ways, I shall not
write again. It is worth considering for a moment,
however, whether the town and county governments
should so often be inconsiderate of each other, or
even antagonistic to each other, as they are in many

cases where one or more towns in rural counties have corporate existences. It is only when town and country are virtually co-extensive that governments of town and country may safely be united in one government—and this is very seldom the case when country towns are concerned. Yet, where a county provides a lot of governmental machinery and then two or three towns inside it provide for themselves similar machinery to do similar work, the costs of government are made high for all concerned. Especially is this the case when the two governing bodies work at cross purposes. And when the town governments proceed, as they sometimes do, on the theory that their only concern is to take care of the town and that what happens to the country outside is no concern of theirs, there is likely to be less of good feeling toward the town than might be desired. There is, indeed, an opportunity both for great reductions of cost and great increase in efficiency in the running of our local machinery of government. It would seem possible for town and county governments actively to co-operate with a decided saving to the taxpayers in many instances; and certainly the hardheaded business men of the country towns have a chance to be of real service to farm taxpayers as well as to town taxpayers by giving some real thought to the simplification of local government, to reducing the expense of it and increasing its efficiency. Business methods in country government would lessen the burdens of taxpayers much more than can any spectacular and newspaper-touted income tax cut Congress is ever likely to make.

THE TOWN WITH A SOUL

The town with a soul, the town that has outgrown the childish dream of more bigness, that has come to concern itself with beauty more than with size, with care for the people already in and about it more than with desire for people elsewhere who might be brought to it, that has moved its boundaries of interest back from the ends of its streets and the pocketbooks of its leading citizens to the farther end of the country lanes and the largest reach of its children's daringest dreams—with the coming of that town will come a deeper love for the soil, a saner pride in neighborhood achievement, a truer conception of the dignity and worth of country life, a finer spirit of brotherhood and of patriotism. That is the town that may be. I like to think of it in the phrases of Vachel Lindsay, who, for all his startling experiments of sound and form, has always seemed to me above all the poets of the community consciousness. Listen to these lines from "The Illinois Village,"

> Who can pass a district school
> Without the hope that there may wait
> Some baby-heart the books shall flame
> With zeal to make his playmates great,
> To make the whole wide village gleam
> A strangely carved celestial gem,
> Eternal in its beauty-light,
> The Artists' town of Bethlehem!

And to these, "On the Building of Springfield,"

> Let not our town be large, remembering
> That little Athens was the Muses' home,
> That Oxford rules the heart of London still,

That Florence gave the Renaissance to Rome.
Say, is my prophecy too fair and far?
I only know, unless her faith be high,
The soul of this, our Nineveh, is doomed,
Our little Babylon will surely die.

And we would not have our little Babylons die.
We would have them become living souls indeed,
drawing their nutriment from the soil, along with
the grass and the trees, and growing into more of
beauty and of goodness as the generations go by.

Chapter XI

THE BODY OF THE TOWN

A COUNTRY TOWN SHOULD BE BEAUTIFUL

It is not on my mind to attempt in these pages any program for civic beautification, to write out any recipe for changing ugly towns to beautiful towns. It is my purpose, instead, merely to plead that some of the town's thought be given to beauty, that the country town, fitting itself into a new and finer country life, unite itself with the country by ties of bodily beauty as well as of spiritual understanding. Our countryside has as one of its great needs the need of more beauty; the town shares this need with the countryside. Indeed, the lack of beauty, as a rule, is greater in the town than in the country. Nature's redemptive efforts have freer play among the fields. If the town is to take its rightful place as the center of country life, it must bring into itself more of the beauty and the charm and the healthfulness of the fields.

For most of all, to make itself attractive and homelike and desirable, the average town needs trees and grass and vines and flowers and the fresh breath of the country air—needs these even more than finer buildings, or statelier monuments, or more city-like streets. And yet, the country town might well give more thought to its architecture and to the effect of that architecture on the town life and the lives of the people who come to town. Let me tell a little about two towns I have seen, an American and an English town:

IF OBEDSTOWN SHOULD GO TO WINDERMERE

No one who has read Mark Twain's *Gilded Age* is likely to have forgotten "Obedstown." The picture he painted of that village is one of those pictures that impress themselves too deeply on the mind for the erasure of early forgetfulness:

You would not know that Obedstown stood on the top of a mountain, for there was nothing to indicate it— but it did; a mountain that stretched abroad over whole counties, ...

The squire's house was a double log cabin, in a state of decay; two or three gaunt hounds lay asleep about the threshold. Rubbish was scattered about the grassless yard; a bench stood near the door with a tin wash-basin on it and a pail of water and a gourd. There was an ash-hopper by the fence, and an iron pot, for soft-soap boiling, near it.

This dwelling constituted one-fifteenth of Obedstown; the other fourteen houses were scattered about among the pine trees and among the cornfields in such a way that a man might stand in the midst of the city and not know but that he was in the country.

Obedstown stands now, as it stood then, on the top of a "mountain" that does not look like a mountain; and it is still a little village with cornfields and woods—and more of woods than of cornfields— coming up close to its doors. The coal Squire Hawkins jubilated over is plentiful about it, even if the copper is not; but the development he foretold has come much more slowly than he expected. There are some four or five hundred people in the town now, a railroad has crept to within a few miles of it, and a good highway has lately put it in touch with the outside world; but the development of the town and of the country about it is still to come.

Obedstown is not a beautiful town. It has improved somewhat since the days of Mark Twain's boyhood; but it has grown, as most American towns have grown, haphazard and at random. A courthouse stands in a square in the middle of it, after our commonplace Southern fashion, and grouped about this square is the usual small town hodgepodge of buildings of all sorts of designs and materials. The courthouse is not of very attractive design, but it is a rather attractive building. It is attractive because of the material of which it is built—a warm, red sandstone quarried close by the town. A few others of the town's more substantial buildings are of this same sandstone, and they save the town from utter drabness. One of them, a little bank building, would attract the eye of the beauty lover even in a great city.

The town may yet have some of the unloveliness it had; but it is not without a touch of the beauty it lacked then.

It is a far cry from Obedstown on the Cumberland Plateau to Windermere in the English Lake Country. A far cry in many ways; for Windermere is beautiful as Obedstown has never dreamed of being beautiful. Of all the little towns I have seen, I should choose Windermere as the most satisfying to the eye of the sojourner. Down by the lake, away from the town proper, tourist-serving folks have put up alien structures that should never have been erected: but Windermere itself is a harmony of building material and of architectural design. The native gray stone, in squared blocks, or oftener in thin and irregular cleavings, is the basis of practically every building, and the effect is so pleasing that one leaves the town wondering why any town can be content to clothe itself in ragged motley.

It is not likely that the builders of Windermere planned, each as he built, "I will help make this village a place of charm and distinction, a place to which for many years men will come gladly"; but that is what those builders accomplished. If they did it merely by the following of a wise tradition and from the impetus of a wholesome impulse, so much the greater is the credit due them.

Obedstown might even yet grow into charm and distinction by deliberate design, might purposely make of itself a town to which for generations men would turn with pleasure and from which they would carry away grateful memories. It would not be an overly hard thing to assure for itself such a future. Let it but determine that every building of importance going up in the town should be of its own rich-hued native stone and should be designed in some sort of harmony with the buildings already there, and soon this isolated and unknown village would find itself acquiring a reputation and drawing visitors unto itself. And from a practical point of view, the thing could be done easily—the stone waits in abundance; the cost to any builder over some other material he might use would be small.

Charm and distinction are not attributes of many American towns. Most of them have grown up, as this town grew, from unlovely beginnings, and have been, without thinking or caring about it, replete with unloveliness all their lives. Deliberate town planning has been a thing almost unknown among us—certainly, the planning for beauty has been; for we have not thought of beauty as a financial asset. Abundant and varied ugliness our small towns have acquired as a matter of course. Yet, little as our thrifty town builders may think of it, beauty would draw the eyes of men to a town—and open for it the pockets of strangers—in America as well as in England or Italy.

A California town with a long, enticing history and a few attractive old Spanish buildings found itself growing into the regulation American town. All kinds of buildings were going up in it and its ancient beauty was being lost in its modern "development." With unusual wisdom the town took thought for its future and decided that its Main Street should not be a mere replica in hodge-podge of a thousand other towns, but that it should be built into a harmony after the old Mission model and tradition. The town is down in the tourist folders now as a beauty spot and thousands journey by it just because it is unique and beautiful.

The dream I had in its streets of a distinctive and

beautiful Obedstown may remain a stranger's idle dream, which the responsible builders of the town will think not worth a dollar of theirs. Like most American villages, Obedstown is not yet concerning itself with the desire for beauty or with plans for the generations yet to be. Yet from a purely financial standpoint it would pay Obedstown to plan and build itself into a town of charm and of individual distinction. And if all the business men of this little town— of any one of a thousand other towns in this land of ours—could be dropped down into the streets of Windermere for a day's rambling, I can not help thinking that a new idea of what a little town can be would quicken the building activities and change the whole thought and character of one American village.

TWO OR THREE OTHER SUGGESTIONS

Thinking of this town and its possibilities for distinction, I am reminded of some others I have seen.

There is N, for example. A little river runs through N, the level land on which the town is built on one side of it, a wooded bluff up which a steep road climbs on the other side. There is a bridge across the little river, and new houses are being put up on the bluff. Most of them are good-looking houses, and they add to the town's appearance. But along the river front, which should be the town's chief attraction, are scattered on both sides pigpens and privies and rubbish dumps; and the beauty one should see from the river bridge is obscured by the unsightliness he cannot miss.

N is the trading center for a good farming section; but N is in no fix to lead that farming country into a larger appreciation of beauty, or order, or self-appreciation, or sanitary foresight.

Far south on the banks of the sluggish Yazoo is another country town. Coming into that town by night across the river, one sees, first of all, the lights along the river side and the reflected lights below in the river's self; and the scene is one of beauty. The traveler is drawn to that town; it holds out to him the promise of the unusual. He crosses the river and the promise ceases to whisper, the prospect to allure; and approaching the town at another time or by another route, there would be nothing out of the ordinary.

Yet what would it not be worth to any town to have all the main approaches to it hinting to the traveler of something alluring and unusual and romantic in the village he was about to enter? What would it not be worth, especially, if the town should fulfill the promise of its approaches and really prove unique and beautiful?

Little towns often think of parks as things pertaining to real cities; but the parking of a town should begin with its growth—not formal and artificial parking in every case; but even oftener the preservation of natural beauty that is about the town. A clump of fine trees, a clear running spring, a shaded pathway, a fine view, are all things worth preserving. Few philanthropists have done a finer thing for their towns than did he who gave to Robert Burns' town of Ayr the delicious walk-way along the bank of its little river. A playground is community wealth, and even the little burg should provide playgrounds for its children. No town should consider itself complete these days without a camping site for passing strangers and a parking place for trading farmers—and these places should not be dump-heaps for tin cans or spaces of muddy bareness. Some towns are planting town forests, and so securing beautiful utilities and dividend-paying attractions. The town gardens so common about British towns might find a place in the economy of some American towns, though they would seem to promise most for the more strictly industrial cities. One thinks of all the crimes that have been perpetrated under the names of monuments and memorials and hesitates to suggest more of them; yet every town should preserve its local history in a tangible way and keep constantly before its people the names and deeds of its worthiest inhabitants, the suggestion of its finest accomplishments. Memorials can be both dignified and simple and need not take always the form of imitative buildings or stereotyped statuary. The community memorial, too, may often be a common possession of town and country, a link to hold them together.

The town that seeks to grow in bodily grace and charm and delight to the senses of men will find abundant ways in which to do it.

THE TOWN IN THE LANDSCAPE

The town is part of the landscape. It should be the crown of the landscape, fitting into it, making the beauties of nature more beautiful by its presence. Yet how often is it anything but—often literally—a blot and a disfigurement on the landscape it should adorn. Let me tell of just one more town, a town that might, alas, be named Legion:

Through lush bluegrass pastures, between fields of knee-high corn and ripening wheat the train ran. Through its window one caught glimpses of attractive farmhouses and ample barns, of orchards and grazing livestock, of hard white roads and clear bright streams.

The train slowed down. It was stopping at a country village. On one side of the track the village was only a row of ramshackle old buildings, a muddy "street" leading out of the main road, beyond it a few neat homes with the green of the grass and trees about them, and still beyond them the wholesome fields again and a flock of sheep grazing on a hill. From the other side of the car one could see half a dozen ugly, rickety, uncared-for shacks; the new iron-fronted shed of a store building, not rickety, but as ugly as any of the wrecks; a mudhole beside the station. The general impression was that of uncleanliness, unthriftiness, and unsightliness. The whole town, as seen from the train, was a blot on the face of the fields.

There are dozens and dozens of such towns—towns unlike this one in every respect but one, perhaps, but very like it in their stark and unashamed ugliness. Every reader has seen them. The town that fits into the country about it as a part of the scheme of things; the town that does not seem some sort of unhealthy excrescence upon the face of the fields instead of their natural completion; the town that does not flaunt ugliness instead of beauty at the passer-by, is the very exceptional town. So used have we become to them that we accept them as matters of course, forget that they need not be, and never once think that their existence is proof that we lack comprehension of the true aim of industry and commerce.

Let no one imagine that our villages are going to be made over into "model towns" to conform to anyone's esthetic ideals, or that they are going to cease to be, first of all, places of business adapted, first of all, to business needs. The town is established to do business. People group themselves into towns because they can do business better so grouped than when scattered abroad. They live in town that they may be convenient to their business, their work. Even the little hamlet of twenty or fifty houses exists for commercial reasons and is dominated by its business houses—dominated by them both as regards its appearance and as regards its habits of life and thought. Our towns are not going to be remade, or even changed, save along business lines and for business ends.

This much may as well be conceded to begin with; but, having conceded it, let us ask ourselves in all seriousness whether good business demands the building of unsightly towns. Then let us in all honesty answer our own question.

A certain type of mind will, of course, answer at once that since these things are they must continue to be, and that they would not have been at all if there had not been a good reason for them. The weed-grown alleys, the spaces of alternate slush and dust about the depot and the courthouse, the unpainted, rat-harboring old firetraps that persist in standing, the brazen unsightliness of "business fronts" that might have been made tasteful—all these to this type of mind are necessary because they are, and must therefore continue to be.

Every town has in it men of this type, and these men are often among the most substantial citizens of the town. But no town has been built by men with such minds. The men who have founded towns and have made them grow have been men of vision— dreamers, if you will. They may have regarded themselves as the most practical and least visionary of men, and they probably have been abundantly practical for all business purposes, but they dreamed dreams and saw visions none the less. It is to men who dream that the world owes its material progress as well as its spiritual advancement; and these men may well ask themselves if country towns need to gather unto themselves so much that is depressing to look at and undesirable to live with. They may ask themselves, as practical men, if weeds and filth and mud and tumbled-down buildings and debauched

architecture and hideous advertising at a town's
front door—or its back door, either—are good business propositions. They may ask themselves, as men
who can see things that are not visible to the bodily
eye, if there are not possible changes that can be
wrought to the great advantage of their own towns.
They may go a bit further, if they are really and
truly "practical" in a big way, and looking to the
ultimate results of things, ask themselves if there
is not something radically wrong with the industry
that produces such abounding ugliness, if not as its
main output, at least as a regular by-product. They
may even ask themselves what effect these squalid
and tasteless things have on the children who grow
up among them, and the men who do business in
and about them, even on the civilization to which
they seem permanently to have attached themselves.

Once asking these questions, there is little doubt of
the answer the practical business men of our towns
will give to them. We Americans are intensely practical people; but we are also confirmed idealists,
dreamers of daring dreams, seers of impossible visions. It is only the dreamer who sees the new thing;
and the man who does the new thing is by that very
proof either himself a dreamer or else a follower of
some dreamer's lead. Nations and cities and little
country towns are built by men of imagination.

It will pay us then, to take time to dream a little
about the country town that might be; to imagine
for a little while what our own town would be like
if it were made fair where it is now unsightly, invit-

ing where it is now forbidding; to plan a little as to how our dreams can be made to become realities.

So to dream, so to imagine, so to plan, will not be a beating of the air; it will be a labor of the most practical sort for some thousands of town officials, town business men, town fathers and mothers. It will be practical labor as well as pleasant exercise because things tangible will come of it.

A TOWN IS AS IT LOOKS

The soul of a town, as of a man, is of more importance than the body. Still in the town, as in the man, soul and body unite and become parts of each other; and even that bodily part which is more surely and purely material is itself of importance. It is worth the time of any town to strive for bodily beauty—at least, for bodily cleanliness and well-being no town should be willing to flaunt ugliness in the faces of its visitors, or to hide unwholesomeness away from its own people. Even the little town should be ashamed to have the things of which this chapter has been complaining. Even the most "practical" town should be willing to give a little thought to the appearances. Even the most economical town should realize that it is cheating its children instead of saving for them when it sends them to a poorly designed schoolhouse in an unplanted schoolyard, and that it is losing trade it should invite when it allows its courthouse halls to become yellowed with tobacco juice, or its ladies' rest-room to smell like a cellar.

The civilization of which the love and cultivation of beauty is not an integral part is necessarily a passing civilization; the town that can achieve only ugliness by its growth will one day be given over without regret to the conquering grass which shall reclaim its misused streets.

Chapter XII

SOME TOWN FOLKS AND THEIR COUNTRY CONTACTS

THE BANKER

In any community the banker is an important and influential man. He occupies a strategic position. Through the gate which he guards practically the whole of the community's business must sooner or later pass in review. His business compels him to know something of every other man's business. His words are listened to with respect, and often they are fateful for good or ill to individuals or to the whole community.

A prominent banker declared recently that most bankers are not good business men, that they lack the courage and the initiative that make men successful in other lines of business, that often they discourage business enterprise and expansion and are content to become gatherers and holders of the money produced by the efforts of more daring and progressive men.

Like any other group characterization, this one is to be accepted only with many exceptions and reservations; but it probably has much truth in it. By the very nature of his business the banker must be a conservative. His position demands that he take no unnecessary risks with his own money or with other people's. Next to integrity itself, caution and self-control are the qualities most demanded in a banker. A community whose financial adviser would be willing to try get-rich-quick schemes for himself or to recommend them to other people would be a community in imminent danger. First of all, a bank must conserve and protect.

Yet even a banker can be too conservative for his community's good, and the charge that bankers tend to become mere money changers and tool gatherers would find evidence to support it in many a country town. It is doubtful if bankers generally have come to appreciate the position they occupy or the responsibility they carry, especially doubtful if the typical banker who deals with country people realizes the opportunity that is his for guiding the business thought of farmers along safe lines. The contact of most bankers with the mass of country people, despite great progress made in recent years, remains too slight and too intermittent. The average farmer still thinks of the bank only as a place to keep his money, when he has money, or to borrow money, when he has to have some more.

In an earlier chapter I told a story about one country banker; let me tell here a little about one in another state.

This man, whom we may call Mr. P, lives in a little Kentucky town. Back in 1921, when the farmers were in the throes of "deflation," and when they seemed to have lost most of their fighting courage along with most of their war-time profits, he decided that it was up to him as a banker to do something to help them get back, if possible, a little of both money and nerve. He began by promoting a get-together meeting of farmers from all over the county to discuss the agricultural situation. A little later a Farm Bureau was organized. Within a year a county farm agent was employed. And all the time Mr. P was visiting farmers here and there over the county, finding out what they were doing, and finding out what their problems were. If he found a farmer with a few cows or a few steers and a bit of uncertainty as to how they should be fed, he would invite that farmer to call at the bank for a bulletin on feeding, a bulletin in which the pertinent paragraphs had been marked so that the farmer could easily get the information he needed. In the spring of 1922, the bank distributed 685 sittings of purebred eggs on the plan outlined in an earlier chapter, and that fall a poultry show was held. At that time Mr. P's county stood tenth in the state in poultry production; today it stands fourth. The next year a few purebred bulls were brought to the county to be placed with farmers who needed and would care for them. In 1924 there was printed in the county paper a letter to Mr. P from a "Small Farmer" who detailed his circumstances and the conditions on the farm, and asked what he could do to get his farm business on a better paying basis. Along with this letter was an offer of four prizes to the four boys or girls in the upper grades of the county's schools who would give the best answers to "Small Farmer's" questions. Fifty-eight boys and girls entered the contest, and twenty-

eight older farmers were sufficiently interested to try
their hand at answering the questions. Haphazard
answers were not given. The co-operation of the
county agent had been secured and each of the contestants received a series of nine lessons on the various farm problems raised by the letter. When the
papers went in to be judged three months after the
contest opened, it was found that the contestants had
written an average of some 20,000 words each in
their answers to questions asked and in the essays
submitted. The prizes offered were a Jersey heifer, a
young sow, a beef heifer, and a radio set. Winner of
the first prize had first choice among these, and so on
down the line. To the general surprise of the big
crowd at the meeting at which the awards were made,
the choices were in the order I have given them.
Another contest of similar nature is in progress as
this is written, and 793 boys and girls are contestants
in it —every one of them, by reason of this fact, a
student of the county's farm problems. This banker,
too, has worked out an application blank for farmers
desiring loans; and when it is filled out Mr. P has a
detailed analysis of that man's farming and what he
is getting from it. "I have known Mr. P to tell a small
farmer who wished to borrow $300 that he could
have the money if he would sell a horse, which was
not needed, and buy another milk cow," writes a man
who has been closely associated with him. "At another
time a loan was made provided the borrower would
sow twice as much clover as had been his custom and
lime a portion of his land."

No other banker might care, or need, to pursue the lines of activity Mr P has followed; but many another country town banker might profit both himself and his community by taking an equally active and intelligent interest in the welfare of the farmers about. For the banker's interest in the prosperity of the farmer is second only to that of the farmer himself; and no other man in town is in such good position to find out just what is wrong with a farmer's business methods or to have his suggestions for improvement of those methods listened to and considered.

Before the banker makes any suggestions, however, it behooves him to be exceedingly careful of his ground. One may be a good banker without knowing much about farming; and if there is any one thing the farmer has had an abundance of, that thing is advice from people who thought they knew more about farming than they really did. Still, the country town banker who does not know something about farming and the particular troubles of farmers may safely be put down as a man wno has neglected one end of his job.

THE MERCHANT

More often even than the banker, more often indeed than any other man in town, the merchant comes in contact with the farmer and the farmer's family; and more than any other man the merchant is likely to be responsible for the attitude of the farmer toward the town. To the store everybody comes; with the storekeeper everybody has dealings. Country folks thinking of "town" usually think first of all of the stores and the people who stay in them.

In 1925 the Retailers' National Council, in co-operation with the business men of those towns, made a survey of three Illinois towns, D, R, and S. This survey was made "to find out what was wrong with D, R, and S, as seen by all the classes of people who make up the town and county and to show the things that should be met and overcome by the business men of the communities in order to make them more prosperous and more wholesome." The results of the survey were published in booklet form by the *National Retail Clothier;* and it would seem that almost any country town merchant could profit by a study of this report. The people in and about each town were asked quite a number of questions about the town and their feelings toward it. Some of these questions were:

How do you feel toward D as a place to trade? If favorable, why? If unfavorable, why?

What do you think of the stores in general?

How could these stores be improved?

What are the best stores in town, and why?

What stores do you like to trade at, and why?

What difficulties do you find in trading here?

What articles do you buy elsewhere because you cannot get them here?

And so on.

There were questions, too, about other features of the town business life; but they need not be considered here.

Tabulation of the reports on these towns shows some differences, naturally; but the points of agreement are more numerous than those of difference, and the report for any one of the towns might be taken as fairly representative of them all. Some of the findings as to D, the first town on the list, may be briefly summarized:

Of the town residents, 53 per cent were favorable to D as a place to trade, 47 per cent unfavorable; of the country residents, 41 per cent favorable, 59 per cent unfavorable. Nearby cities were mentioned as better places to trade. Convenience had much to do with the preference of the country people for going elsewhere. As to the stores themselves, the verdict of the country people was more favorable than that of the town people. The major complaints of both were practically the same, too high prices, lack of variety and—poor clerk service! The dry goods stores especially were complained of because of the "general indolence, discourtesy, slow attention, and lack of ability of the clerks." Fewer stores, improved appearance of stores, periodic advertising, quicker turnover and smaller profits, were among the numerous suggestions for improvement. Numerous articles, men and women's clothing in particular, were bought out of town because local merchants did not have the kind or quality desired. A goodly number found difficulty in getting shoes to fit in the local stores.

The same general line of replies came to the questionnaire for R; but at that town the suggestion for improvement made by the second largest num-

ber of country people was that the stores be kept
open in the evening during the busy season on the
farm.

The general trend of the replies, in short, seemed
to indicate that the farmers about these three towns
felt that the merchants expected them to trade there
principally because of convenience, and that these
merchants were offering few inducements in the way
of price, quality of goods handled, efficiency of service, or thought of the countryman's convenience,
to hold the farmer trade. The result was a farmer
trade that went habitually to larger places for certain goods, and preferred to buy still other things at
those places when it was not too inconvenient to
do so.

Now, there was a time when the average farmer
pretty nearly had to trade at his local town; but
that time has passed in most sections and is passing
in others. The farmer's buying territory has been
greatly extended by the mail order house, the parcel
post, and the automobile. The country town merchant who tries to hold farmer trade by virtue of
propinquity only, and who does not try to give
the farmer as low prices, as desirable goods, and as
courteous service as that farmer can get elsewhere,
is not likely to hold the country trade. Nor is he
likely to increase the farmer's affection for the town
or to help develop in the country districts that feeling of loyalty to the larger community of town and
country which both town and country so much need.

The merchant stands on one side of the counter

and the farmer on the other, not when the farmer buys only, but when he sells. The same merchant may not be—though he often is—both buyer from and seller to the farmer; but both functions will be performed by some of the town's merchants. And those merchants, once they give the impression that they are trying to give the farmer as good bargains in buying as anyone else can give him and trying to pay or secure for him a fair price for what he has to sell, can do more in most cases than can any other group of equal size to promote good feeling and confidence between town and country.

THE EDITOR

Some years ago I was quite a bit younger then than I am now, and at that era of the world it happened that I wrote the resolutions for a State Farmers' Convention. Among those resolutions was one addressed to the editors of the states' county papers asking them to publish more farm news and to give more attention in their columns to the things country people were doing, and less to matters of no real importance to their communities.

I know now that it would have been more appropriate for me to have addressed that resolution to the farmers there assembled and to have urged them to get in closer touch with their local newspapers; but for all that, the complaint against the papers was justifiable. It would be justifiable in many cases today, though less generally so than at that time.

A good local newspaper is one of the most effective of town builders. Too often, however, the local newspaper is a town booster instead of a town builder—and there is a world of difference between the two. The newspaper tradition, in fact, has come to be that of boosting; the paper is expected to tell what a wonderful town its town is and often to hand out to its readers whatever ballyhoo the Chamber of Commerce or the Merchants' Association may turn out; it is expected always to tell the things that will "help the town grow," and to advise the farmers of their duty to trade at home. All of which is well enough if kept within bounds and matched with a willingness to tell unpleasant truths about local affairs when such truth-telling is necessary, and with the courage to think more of subscribers' interests than of an advertiser's wishes when the two conflict. Lacking courage and conviction, the local paper becomes a shoddy, ineffectual thing and soon ceases to have much influence on the public mind or on public policy. With courage, conviction, and understanding, the editor often can do more than any other one man to promote the welfare of the town and its territory. The editor has the advantage of being able to get the full effect of repetition. He can tell his tale over and over—"Line upon line, precept upon precept"—and after awhile the line and precept become impressed on the public mind.

Certainly the editor, of all men, is in position to help make one community of town and surrounding country. He can carry the message of the town to the country home; can bring understanding of farm conditions right to the town's hearthsides. Especially if he is country bred, or if he has real knowledge of farm life, can he become the farmer's potent advocate as well as the farmer's trusted adviser. The opportunity offered by the country newspaper office to the young man whose desire for service and for a growing respect and appreciation exceeds his desire for wealth or spectacular success seems to be an opportunity scarcely excelled anywhere, and an opportunity, despite the spreading distribution of the great city dailies, probably greater than ever before.

True, it is the exceptional case in which the relations between the local editor and the masses of country people are as close as they should be. The editor is not likely to know country people as well as he does town people, or to see them as often. The men with whom he does most of his business and from whom he gets most of his money are townsmen. Generally, too, he will get much less of support and co-operation and understanding than he is justly entitled to from country folks. To many farmers the local paper is still an acquaintance only—not yet a friend despite its frequent visits. There is often the feeling that the paper is a special pleader for the town, and that it is little concerned with country doings or country interests. Fortunate indeed is the country town editor who has made his country folks think of his paper as their chronicler, their forum, their spokesman. Farmers, generally speaking, could do much to make their paper this desirable thing; and when it so became they would have a real affection for it. But it is seldom they will take the initiative in doing it; the editor himself must take the first steps, make the beginnings. Farmers' meetings, farm activities, must come to be real news to him; farm homes must come to know him as something more than a name. If he is not the man to find pleasure in rural contacts, or to see dignity and importance in country doings, he can scarcely hope either to see things from the country viewpoint or to impress his own point of view upon the country mind.

THE LABORING MAN

Despite the effort to form a Farmer-Labor Party and so to unite farmers and urban workers for political action, it is doubtful if the farmers of the United States and union labor have ever been less in sympathy or have less understood each other. During the post-war period of deflation—which came first of all to the farmer and still lingers with him— farmers saw laboring men, especially the members of certain strongly entrenched unions, getting wages entirely out of proportion to the wages received by the farmers themselves. They even saw some of these laboring men asking for, and actually getting, wage increases while the returns from farm work were all the time getting smaller. Naturally this bred resentment. Some farmers, indeed, persuaded themselves, or were persuaded, that most of their troubles were due to the high wages city workers were getting.

This was, of course, unreasonable. Those workingmen got high wages because the industries of which they were a part were making big profits. This, except in the case of such public-service employees as the railroad men who got high wages, because they were in position to make the whole public pay those wages. The farmer, meanwhile, found himself unable to pay competing wages to his employees, or to secure equal pay for his own labor. He was a "sweated" laborer during this period; but the urban workingman did not appreciate that fact, seemingly, any more than the farmer appreciated the fact that other industries were paying high wages when he could not because those industries were making big profits, and that these profits and not the high wages were what was hurting him. Certainly, the average farmer has had little sympathy these past few years with striking coal miners, protesting railroad workers, or indeed with any effort of labor to raise or maintain wages.

Yet despite this estrangement, farmer and laboring men have certain important interests in common. It is to the interest of the laboring man that the farmer be prosperous; for the farmer is still the largest single consumer. Practically any basic industry can afford to lose any other single market it has rather than the farm market. For two or three years now, all other industries have seemed to prosper while farming remained unprofitable; but any long continued depression on the farm is going to close down factories and throw men out of employment. Steady employment means more to the laboring man in town than does cheap food; and always the laboring man needs to remember in connection with his grocery bill that only a fraction of it gets back to the farmer. Equally, the farmer is interested in steady employment and good wages for the city laborer. Only when the workers are getting well filled pay envelopes will the farmer have a good market for what he raises. Most wage struggles—not all of them—are struggles on the part of the employers to retain more of the returns of an industry as profits and on the part of the employees to secure more of those proceeds in the form of wages. The farmer's interests, in such cases, are with the wage earners— a reasonable degree of prosperity for the many means more to him than does an intensified prosperity for the few. He wants a great number of people able to buy liberal quantities of food.

The efforts of the farmer to secure more for his products—especially his efforts to secure, through co-operative marketing or otherwise, a larger share of the "consumer's dollar"—are primarily efforts to get better pay for his work. It is a common saying that the farmer is both laborer and capitalist. It is also a true saying; but the laboring man needs to remember, as does the farmer himself, that the typical farmer is more laborer than capitalist. The average capital invested per farm in 1920 was $12,084. Farm values had shrunk until economists estimated it at only $10,000 in 1925; and the estimate was certainly a liberal one. This means that the average farmer gets only $500 to $600 a year as interest on his investment. The rest of what he gets is wages for his work and pay for his managerial ability. These wages and this pay have been very small these latter years—not as small as the farmer generally thinks they are, but smaller than the man off the farm generally realizes. The city worker wishes to buy his food as cheaply as he can; but he is not desirous, if he is a wise man, that the country's largest group of workers should work for less than a living wage. He needs to keep this in mind when he thinks about farmer organizations and about other efforts of farmers to improve their conditions; and he needs to remember, too, that the experienced farmer is a skilled workman, comparable in his technical knowledge and ability to the trained machinist or builder. Some farm workers there are who can only be classed as unskilled labor; but the number of them is much smaller than the man who thinks "anybody can farm" would imagine. Anybody can work on a farm; but it takes just as much of special knowledge and particular skill to do good work and profitable work on a farm as it does in any of the skilled trades.

The interests of farmers and of workingmen in other industries coincide oftener than they conflict.

THE PROFESSIONAL MAN

The professional man—the preacher, the teacher, the doctor, the lawyer—is in position to be something more than a specialist who gives the community the benefit of his particular knowledge and skill. True, it is to be said for him that if he does well this one thing he serves well his town and his time; but even so there is another opportunity for him. His is the chance to be the disinterested student of business and economic conditions and problems, and from these studies to become the capable and impartial umpire in business and economic disputes and conflicts. To make this study, to observe and think along these lines sufficiently to make himself a judge and a mediator, of course, require that he have leisure time—which many professional men do not have—and also that he have a taste for study, a liking for his fellow men, and a love for abstract justice—things which also some professional men may not have. Many have them, however, in greater or less degree; and these men can be of wonderful help in bringing town and country to an understanding and a working agreement. For all of them—the teacher, possibly, at times excepted—deal with both town and country people; and all of them owe it to their country clients or patrons to know something of the country, not from the outside only, but from the inside as well.

Professional men are often leaders in civic affairs, in the town's organizations and its community activities. I doubt if it is exaggerating much to say that in most towns they are the leaders. Even the business men's club will often have as its spokesman the public-minded lawyer or doctor or preacher. This man has learned the town, the things it wishes, the things it aspires to do, and knows how to lead it and how to speak for it. He can do the same things for the country. And why should he not?

Yet preachers preach, even in country churches, who have more knowledge of the shepherds of Judea

than of the stockmen of their own state, more acquaintance with the grapes of Eschol than with the
troubles of the orchardists in their own land. The
ignorance of many teachers about fundamentals of
agriculture, or the basic facts of country life is piti-
ful. The most capable and distinguished lawyers,
or doctors, or engineers of a little city will too often
be found out of sympathy or understanding with
the family on the little farm. And just as often, and
just because of an equal lack of understanding, the
man on the farm thinks of these men with no adequate appreciation of their value to him or to the
community.

THE TOWN HOUSEKEEPER

If anybody in town has valid cause of complaint
against the farmer, the housekeeper who buys his
products is that person. She is of all people least
likely to be enthusiastic over the "honest farmer," or
to pity the "down-trodden agriculturist." For it is
she who knows better than anyone else—unless it be
the produce dealer—the undesirability of a lot of
stuff the farmer sends to town.

Often the housewife thinks she has reason to
complain of the farmer because of the high prices
she has to pay for what he produces; but it is seldom
that she has. It is the very exceptional case when the
farmer has any final voice in the fixing of the retail
prices of farm products—or of wholesale prices,
either, for that matter; and as I have said above, he
gets in most cases only a fraction of what the con-

sumer pays for them. Of the dollar the housekeeper pays for the produce of American farms, less than 40 cent on the average goes to the farmer. Even for things that reach her in almost their natural condition—fruits, vegetables, milk, etc.,—he often gets less than this.

What she has just cause to complain about is that he is so often indifferent to the quality of what he sends to market. She has found, too, that he adds deception to his carelessness at times. The housekeeper in the little town is more likely to suffer from these failings of the farmer than is the housekeeper in the large cities. Her dealings with him are more nearly direct; she gets in many cases a less thoroughly standardized and commercialized product. She still knows something about bad country butter, ancestral eggs, plated barrels of apples, unsorted potatoes, underfed chickens. Not all the bad or poorly prepared foodstuffs she gets are to be blamed on the farmer; the dealer is not always immaculate; but the farmer has his due share of the blame justly to bear.

In some cases the farmer is guilty of actual dishonesty in the preparation of his products for the market. More often he is guilty only of slipshod and careless methods of production and preparation and of ignorance of market requirements. He has in too many cases given no real thought to the putting of his goods on the market in attractive shape and in prime condition. The country over, as a matter of fact, he is just beginning to learn that there is profit in sending to market a product of uniform and dependable quality. The town housekeeper, for this reason if for no other, should be the friend of farmer co-operation, the advocate of the countryman's co-operative marketing associations. From these organizations she will get a standardized product and a dependable one; no co-operative would be so foolish at this late date as to put its brand on a product it did not believe to be of desirable quality. If the housekeeper should have to pay a little more—which is usually not the case—for this standardized product, she would still find it really cheaper than one that could not be depended upon; and if—as is usually the case —the farmer should by reason of his marketing association get a little more for his product he would be encouraged to produce more liberally and to think more of quality. And so the housekeeper would be the gainer all around.

The woman who buys food for her family wishes to buy that food cheaply; the man who grows food products to sell wishes to get all he can for them. That old conflict of buyer and seller will remain. It is not to the buyer's interest, however, that the producer get so little for his product as to discourage production of it; nor is it to the producer's interest that the consumer have to pay so much as to discourage consumption. Both of them are interested in making the pathways of distribution short and easy and the costs of distribution small; and both of them are interested in any method or device or practice that helps to give the consumer products of quality and of dependable reputation. Purchasing housekeepers will soon come to realize that the organization of farmers for co-operative marketing is a good thing for them. Some day, too, these housekeepers may come to organize for co-operative buying, and that will be a good thing for the farmers.

But that is another story. The town housekeeper, whether she deals directly with the farmer or buys his products through the usual channels of trade, will be serving best her own interests and his by insisting that when his products come to her they be not only what they pretend to be, but also that they come to her in shape to be used with the minimum of waste and loss and trouble.

Chapter XIII

THE FINER FUTURE THROUGH
CAREFUL PLANNING

WHY WE ARE WHAT WE ARE

It has well been said that the agriculture of this country is a sort of Topsy—it has "just growed" as chance or circumstance might indicate or determine. Development has followed the lines of least resistance. Thought of as a plant, agriculture is a sprawling bunch of crabgrass, reaching and rooting haphazardly where it finds easiest opportunity, rather than an upstanding stalk of corn growing into a predictable form and fruitage. The country at large, the farmers themselves, have had no definite ideal of what American agriculture should be like, or what it should accomplish. As Prof. Walton H. Hamilton has said:

"No one ever intended that cotton planting, or wheat growing, or dairy farming should be organized as it is today. If each farmer has to make his plans in the dark with little knowledge of what others are doing, and if matters of interest will get lost in the shuffle, it is not because someone has willed it that way. If the incidence of neglected organization appears in inadequate income, in a denial of too many of the good things of life to too many people dependent upon agriculture, in the restrictions of opportunities for development to farm children, it is because a neglect of the organization of agricultural industries has left them beyond the pale of man's conscious control."

If this is true of agriculture, it is equally true of agriculture's trading place, the country town. The towns of America have not grown up with so much of physical ugliness and squalor, so much of spiritual smugness and shortsightedness, so little of comprehension as to their place in the scheme of things and their relationship to the country about them, because anyone has willed it so, or because of any evil designs on the part of anybody. They, like the country, have developed along the lines of least resistance, have been guided in their development chiefly by habit and tradition, have become what they are mainly because they did not seek to become anything in particular.

With both town and country, much of this pragmatic and experimental development has been inevitable. Life is an experimental process for industries and for settlements as well as for individuals. It has been, and remains, beyond the power of any person or group of persons to say that dairy farming, for example, should be so conducted as to result in a certain type of farm, of farmer, or of business organization; or to say that a certain group of towns should come to look exactly a certain way and to function in exactly a certain manner. The world has not been run that way—and it is not likely to be so run.

Indeed, there will not be wanting men who will

say that things are what they are simply because they had to be just about that way—that the development of agriculture, of the countryside, of the country town, has been determined by the operation of economic forces and natural laws, and that all the planning and forethought in the world would not have changed things appreciably. These men believe that periodic overproductions of wheat and cotton and pigs and butterfat have been inevitable—decreed by some sort of impersonal fate—and that inevitably along with them have come periods of agricultural distress, unpainted country dwellings, overworked farm women, disconsolate breakings-up of farm homes. These men think too, that the fierce-fronted "business blocks" of little towns had to be, and the hard-fisted policies of some country banks, and the increasing contempt for the backwoods people of certain classes of town citizenship.

With people who think this way, this book has no concern, as they can have none with it. It is addressed, instead, to the men and women who realize that all human industries and all human surroundings are what humanity makes them; who have seen that economic laws are not forces of nature but merely workings of human desire; who believe that mankind can learn from experience to do things better than it has been used to doing them. All these people will agree with me that it is possible for both country life and town life to be made finer and fuller than they now are, and that while none of us is going to be able to take either town or country and mould it exactly to his heart's desire, it is possible for even a few of us, working together, to accomplish something toward that end. All who have this faith may do well to consider for a little how town and country can be led to co-operate for mutual benefit and mutual improvement.

"AS A COMMUNITY THINKETH"

Some of the things towns or townsmen have to bring the town closer to the country about it and help to promote the interests of country dwellers have been told in preceding chapters. Some of the things that might be done have been suggested. It is worth noting, however, that in no case mentioned has there been any comprehensive program of town and country co-operation, or any specific goal fixed for attainment by either town or country. Some fine things have been accomplished both by community and by local effort. Every one of the incidents detailed might be duplicated time and again. Every one of them might well be so adapted as to become a worth-while model for imitation in other communities; but of no town or county of which I have knowledge can it justly be said that it has the vision of the thing it wishes to become or any practical plan for making itself what it would like it be.

This will come in time, let us believe—to a farming community here, perhaps, a town elsewhere, after awhile to a town and its farming community. And when it shall come both to a town and to the country about that town there will almost certainly be

developments and achievements that will make anything yet accomplished along the line of purposeful
community building in this land of ours seem a little
thing. For if our country districts and our country
towns owe their faults and their shortcomings chiefly
to lack of thought and of foresight and of the community mind, thought and the lessons of experience
and co-ordinated effort can work great changes.

The temptation to try to outline a program of community development for a farming district and its
town is with me, but I know it is a temptation to
be resisted. No community is going to get any practical and workable plan until it develops that plan
for itself out of an understanding of its own needs
and its consciousness of its own desires. Anyone who
may be going about with ready-made ideals for other
folks is carrying around a possibly valuable, but a
certainly unsalable commodity.

Some progress, I think, is being made along the
line of community planning. The feeling is abroad in
the land that the agriculture of a county by taking
thought can add to its height, and its breadth, and
its depth. On my desk as I write are half a dozen
programs of agricultural development for as many
counties or farming districts. These programs have
been worked out by various State Divisions of Agricultural Extension in co-operation with the farmers—
sometimes the farmers and the business men—of
the territories to which they apply. Generally speaking, they are definite and practical. They aim at
something tangible and plan to accomplish certain

things within a certain time. All of them, to my thinking, are too much in the nature of made-up affairs, fashioned for and offered to the farmers by men who think they know what the farmers need— too much of the official headquarters and too little of the locality have gone into their making. Still, there is not one of them but that is worthy of being carried out, not one of them but offers a good working plan for its territory to start with. They represent much of actual achievement and more of promise. They show that a community consciousness is abroad in the land.

Some country towns, too, are taking thought of their future, and beginning to think of their future otherwise than in terms of growth. Slowly, perhaps, but surely, the understanding that a town may need to do other things than get bigger—indeed, it may need some other things so much worse that increase in size is not a thing to be desired at all for the time being—is making its way through the collective small town mind. Belief in the possibility of better towns, and of a better countryside, both made better by deliberate planning and working to that end, may not yet be general, but it is widely scattered.

This nation, for example, is just at the beginning of a development which is going to mean as much to the farm folks and work as great changes in country life as did the development of the automobile and the consequent era of quick transportation. The American farm, the American countryside, are going to be electrified. Electric light and electric mechanical power are going to brighten the farmer's home and

to make easier scores of the farmer's, and hundreds
of the farm woman's tasks. Two or three decades
from now life in the typical farm home will be very
different, by reason of this very fact, from what it
is today. The women of the farm especially will be
able to avoid an immense amount of unpleasant mus-
cular exertion that is now necessary; and they will
gain correspondingly in comfort and leisure. All that
this new development will mean to country life, no
one can now foresee; but even now it is evident that
it will make possible in thousands of country homes a
graciousness, and a spaciousness now impossible because of the demands of daily tasks on the family's
time and energy. Even now this thing is taking place;
and it is taking place mostly just as chance and circumstance may determine. A few State Divisions of
Extension are making some study of it, a few of the
big power companies; but where is the city or the
town that has given thought to the electrification
of its own countryside, that is trying to hasten the
coming of the better day electrification will bring, or
trying to guide the development along the safest
and most productive lines?

Yet what a wonderful opportunity for the planning of the larger community of town and country,
and for the broader co-operation of town and country along the lines of mutual advancement waits
here!

WHEN TOWN AND COUNTRY PLAN TOGETHER

It is well for the town to work for the country—
for it to appreciate the importance of the country to

it and set itself to help the country prosper and progress; but it is better for it to work with the country—for it to agree with the country on what needs
to be done in both town and country and then, with
interests harmonized and efforts co-ordinated as
nearly as may be, for the townsmen to unite with
the farmers in bringing about the things desired.
Effectively to secure this unity of purpose and action,
will require in most cases a threefold effort. The
farming district—or its wisest and most unselfish
members—must work out a program of progress for
it; the best minds of the town must do the same
thing for the town; and then the sanest of the country leaders and the soundest of the town's thinkers
must in joint session modify and adjust the two
programs until they fit together and become a part
of each other. Then, and not until then, will it be
time to appeal to town and country alike to come
together, and feel together, and work together, and
together to benefit and improve themselves.

I do not mean by this, of course, that no joint
effort of town and country is to be made until a full
and final program of both town and country development has been worked out, or that the platform on
which town and country are asked to get together
must be one of many planks. Joint effort may be
asked for, and had, in some cases to accomplish but
a single thing. The point is that the joint appeal and
the joint effort should come as a result of joint consideration and discussion. Usually, perhaps, it will
be well if a broad general idea of the future sought

204 FUTURE THROUGH PLANNING

for can be in the minds of the leaders, even though the immediate program may concern itself with only a phase or two of that program; but all this is to be determined by local thought and feeling. The essential thing is that there be faith in the ability of a community, as of a man, to "make something of itself," and that there be the ambition and confidence that will then put the community to work at its noble task.

Chapter XIV

AND IN CONCLUSION

AGRICULTURE IN AN INDUSTRIAL STATE

The United States, so long predominantly agricultural, has become predominantly industrial. Within a generation we have seen the preponderance of population, of wealth, of power, pass from the country to the city. And all the time the cityward trend of people, of wealth, and of power continues. The farmer goes more and more definitely into the minority.

No turning back of this tide is to be expected, though a slowing-up of it is not unlikely. Advancing civilization, as it increases the farmer's ability to produce, makes steadily smaller the comparative number of people needed on the farms. A generation, a century, from now there is every reason to believe that one farm, one farmer, will produce more food, be able to feed more people off the farm, than at present. The country may as well accept its future of decreasing numbers and decreasing political power as compared with the cities.

This does not mean that the farm and the farmer will become of less importance in the scheme of national existence, or that the farmer can be treated with less consideration than formerly. The farmer still remains the essential man; the products of his labor the essential products. However great and

numerous our cities may become, they must be fed;
and they are going to continue to be fed—all dreams
of synthetic foods notwithstanding—on the products
of the soil. In the future as in the past, their living
must come from the farmer's hands.

As the proportionate number of city dwellers to
country dwellers increases there will come, too, an
increasing respect for the farmer, an increasing recognition of his place as the key man in the structure
of civilization. His welfare will come to be more and
more a matter of concern to thoughtful people off
the farms. As long as the nation had more farmers
than it really needed, indifference to their welfare
might not prove disastrous. With the possibility of a
scarcity of farmers, and a corresponding scarcity
of food, any excessive drift away from the land, any
checking of production because of unprofitable returns to the producer, will make even the most ignorant and indifferent tremble. For this nation must
continue to feed itself. Imports of foodstuffs there
will be, of course, as there are now; but the United
States is not going to drift into the position England
now occupies and become a nation that gets most of
its living abroad while it concerns itself chiefly with
manufacture and commerce. It dares not get into such
position. The American farmer will likely gain in
economic power as the years go by. It is not impossible that agriculture may yet come to be the coddled
favorite of the state, as manufacturing has been, and
that "infant industries" of the farm may come to be
fattened at the expense of other industries. Not im-

possible, though it is to be hoped that this will not happen, and that agriculture will be allowed to get along without special favors and with only a square deal. Any other policy will be certain to bring complications and trouble in its train, just as the continued governmental papping of industries that should have been separated from the bottle and the crib long ago has brought about, or at least intensified, many of the social problems over which the nation now vexes its brain.

THE PATH THAT LEADS TO DISASTER

All this is taking for granted that agriculture is to remain an independent, self-respecting, respected and profit-paying occupation. There is another path the nation might follow, another line of agricultural policy it might pursue. Agriculture might be definitely assigned to an inferior rank as compared with other industries, a peasant system of agriculture might be developed, the land passing into the hands of absentee owners, the work of tending that land being assigned to the least progressive and aspiring of the country's citizenship. There are those, seemingly, who would be willing for the country to adopt this policy toward its agriculture; but the nation is not likely to walk in this path. If it should so decide, all discussion of agricultural advancement, of country life improvement, of country town development, would be in vain, and for the nation itself there would be but one inevitable destiny. Great cities might be built up under such a policy, and a wonderful urban civilization. The thing has been done in other lands and in other times; but always with the same result. When the cities reached a certain stage of magnificence and top-heaviness, the country a certain stage of poverty and ignorance and political insignificance, the structure resting on that unsound foundation of poverty and ignorance and weakness toppled and fell.

Let the cities of any land draw into themselves too much of the wealth and intelligence and aspiration of that land, and those cities are doomed. The face of the earth is littered with ruins of broken and fallen civilization, every one of them, so far as we know or have reason to believe, a civilization in which the cities gathered wealth and acquired culture and waxed strong and beautiful and proud, while their food was provided for them by countrymen far inferior in knowledge, in understanding, and in opportunity.

This thing must not happen in America.

THE COUNTRYSIDE OF THE FUTURE

Instead, there must be developed in this country a rural civilization equal to, and integrated with, the civilization of the city. For the man on the farm, life must be made equally pleasant, labor equally profitable, with the life and labor of the man in town. The material blessings of the city must extend themselves into the country. Whatever cultural opportunity the city holds must be open to the youth of the farm. There must be convenience and comfort and beauty and the lightening of labor in the country home as well as in the city apartment. The path to knowledge

and to accomplishment and to power must be open
before the feet of childhood from every farmyard
gate. Only so can the future of the nation be assured.

The thing, too, is possible—not easy of achievement, of course, but within the bounds of practi-
cability. Right here, in the very fields present-day
farmers work, in the very homes they live in, the
very roads they travel, may be developed a finer and
richer country life than the world has yet known—
a life rich not only in the material things that contribute to bodily satisfaction, but richer still in the
things that uplift the hearts and inspire the souls
of men.

This will yet be a land of well tilled fields, of fields
that do not wash away or grow poorer with their
tending, but that become more productive year by
year. The scrub animal will be banished from our
barnyards, the unsightly and uncomfortable farm
home from our country landscapes. To the farm
worker will come a more adequate return than he
has yet had for the labor he performs; to agriculture itself will come a new self-respect, a new
strength, a new determination to uphold its rights
by its own strength and to dignify its votaries by
the things it accomplishes. We shall see—some of us
who are now living—an agriculture organized to do
business in a business way, and a tremendous economic force because of that organization. A home-
owning and a home-loving agriculture this will be—
the farm homes owned by the people who live in
them, loved because of their comfort and beauty,

cherished because of the love that has gone into their making and their keeping. This farm community, too, will be a community with sufficient knowledge to put even its little streams to work for it, to grow forests where crops cannot profitably be raised, to bring the science of the world to its service, to keep itself so clean and so wholesome that typhoid and malaria and hookworm disease and the other "country diseases" will become but evil memories. Above all, this farming community will have such desire for knowledge, such respect for the rights of the humblest, that it will think it a crime to let one child grow up without the benefits of a good school, without books to read, without the opportunity to investigate and experiment and find out things for himself.

This—let us believe—is the future in store for the American farmer and the American countryside. It is a future, however, that will not come by chance or by destiny; it will be realized only as the result of arduous, intelligent, and unselfish labor on the part of many men. In the making of it the country town must have a large part.

AND THE TOWN WILL BE PART OF IT

For the country town is to be an integral part of this finer rural civilization we are to develop. Out amid the more fruitful fields are to stand more beautiful towns; and these towns are not to be set off or divided from the fields and the workers in the fields, as so many of them now seem to be, but to be

joined to and united with the country in myriad
ways. The roads will run out into the country from
the town, and the wires carrying light and power,
and the services of the town's business and professional men; and there will go out also sympathy and
understanding and the realization of brotherhood.

The country town can have only such future as
the countryside may have. Richer and more beautiful
towns can be built only as the country becomes richer
and more beautiful. A town may, perchance, enjoy
an ephemeral prosperity from the exploitation of the
country about it; but ephemeral such prosperity is
bound to be. Its roots are in stony ground; and when
they have drained the little moisture from the thin
soil, the top they support must wither and die.

Every advance of a country district means the possibility of—nay, almost the certainty of—a corresponding advance on the part of the town that ministers to that particular district. Every improvement
in physical structure, in business methods, in spiritual tolerance and understanding, in any country town
carries with it the promise of a corresponding improvement in the appearance, or the practices, or the
spirit of the country about it. "They twain are one
flesh."

To vision the country of today or of tomorrow
as a thing of the fields and woods and farmsteads
only, is to vision it incompletely. An essential part
of that country is the town in the midst of fields and
woods, with its shops and stores, its streets and
spires, its connecting links of railway and postoffice

and telegraph booth to join its country to all the far-off lands. To think of the agriculture of the future as merely a matter of growing crops and feeding stocks, is to think of it altogether inadequately. These things the farmer can do out in his fields and his barns; but his farming compels him also to come to market, and to go to the bank, and to get the news, and to keep in touch with the doings of the world; and he does these things through the medium of his town. Merchant and banker, editor and teacher, track layer and telephone girl, all help him with his farming. If they fail him, he will farm less efficiently and with less profit.

They will not fail him once they have come to understand that he and they are all parts of the same community of interest—that whoever and whatever belongs to the country town is part of the country; and that he who would bring better things to any country town can labor most effectively to that end by helping the country about that town to find and do better things for itself.

www.ingramcontent.com/pod-product-compliance
Lightning Source LLC
Chambersburg PA
CBHW021902020426
42334CB00013B/444